Louisiana Piney Woods
Oil Boom

The rumble started deep underground. The rig crew stopped what they were doing and listened. The well floor began to shake, and oil gushed out of the drill hole, drenching the rig floor, drawworks, boilers, and five wide-eyed floor hands. It was a cool March day in 1925. Crude oil boiled to the surface for an hour before upwelling sand choked off the flow, but that hour forever changed life in Tullos, Urania, and Olla. It unleashed the might of the hydrocarbon atom. (Photograph by Carla Hallmark)

Louisiana Piney Woods
Oil Boom

Jon L. Gibson

PELICAN PUBLISHING COMPANY
GRETNA 2019

The word "Pelican" and the depiction of a pelican are
trademarks of Pelican Publishing Company, Inc., and are
registered in the U.S. Patent and Trademark Office.

Library of Congress Cataloging-in-Publication Data

Names: Gibson, Jon L., author.
Title: Louisiana Piney Woods oil boom / Jon L. Gibson.
Description: Gretna [Louisiana] : Pelican Publishing Company, 2018. |
    Includes bibliographical references.
Identifiers: LCCN 2018027788 | ISBN 9781455624553 (pbk. : alk. paper) |
    ISBN 9781455624560 (ebook)
Subjects: LCSH: Petroleum workers—Louisiana—La Salle Parish—
    History—20th century. | Oil fields—Louisiana—La Salle Parish—
    History—20th century. | Petroleum industry and trade—Louisiana—
    La Salle Parish—History—20th century.
Classification: LCC HD8039.P42 U64 2018 | DDC 338.2/7280976375—
    dc23 LC record available at https://lccn.loc.gov/2018027788

Printed in the United States of America
Published by Pelican Publishing Company, Inc.
1000 Burmaster Street, Gretna, Louisiana 70053
www.pelicanpub.com

To Juanita Fife Wall

"Lord, the mud! It was hub deep to the wagons and belly deep to the mules." – Joe Hargrove, 1983. James "Jick" Justiss's mule team bogged down in El Dorado, Arkansas. (Photograph courtesy of Jennifer Loe, Justiss Oil Company)

Contents

Preface

Close to a trillion barrels of crude oil have been siphoned from subterranean America since Col. Edwin Drake drilled the first commercial oil well, a twenty-barrel-a-day producer at Titusville in northwestern Pennsylvania in 1859 (Darrah 1972). Drake's well fueled a frenzied search for oil across the continent bringing technological innovation, a unique lifeway, colorful language, and — for some risk-takers — unimagined wealth. Oil-based culture grafted itself onto a sleepy America creating welcomed jobs, higher wages, and business opportunities, but it often came with behavior reminiscent of the Wild West during the gold rush. Cultural bipolarity resulted.

Occasionally, itinerant oil people and native townspeople clashed outright, but most of the time, the factions simply went their separate ways or interacted in neutral. Often, the cultural schism was not as much about oil people versus townspeople as about oil people themselves and their nocturnal versus daylight demeanor. Many oil-field workers, or "hardhats," were veterans of flagging strikes nearby, while others were local farmhands or "flatheads-rosinbellies." They worked hard during the day and played hard after dark. The real "saltwaters" in early oil booms were the seedy opportunists — the hijackers, swindlers, card sharks, loan sharks, bootleggers, drug dealers, and "oil field doves" — who followed the strikes looking for a quick buck.

Texas, Oklahoma, Arkansas, and Louisiana were among the states that found themselves in the vanguard of early oil exploration (Franks 1980; Franks and Lambert 1982; Rister 1949; Rundell 1977). Scores of major and minor discoveries were made in the decade before and several decades after the turn of the twentieth century, the age of the oil boom.

Oklahoma's oil veins were recognized as early as 1859 but remained undeveloped because roads and rails were lacking and the federal Dawes and Curtis acts stifled drilling on Native American land where early shows of oil had been discovered. It was not until 1897 that the Bartlesville-Dewey field was proved (Franks 1980; Franks et al. 1981; Rister 1949). Other booms quickly followed: Red

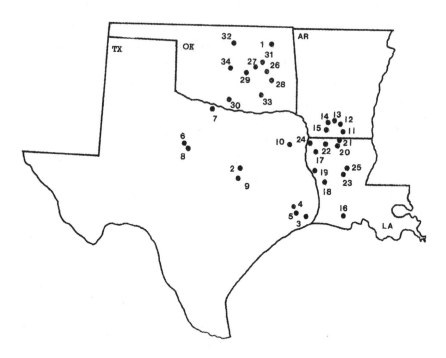

Locations of early oil fields in Arkansas, Louisiana, Oklahoma, and Texas. 1. Bartlesville, Oklahoma; 2. Corsicana, Texas; 3. Spindletop, Texas; 4. Saratoga, Texas; 5. Sour Lake, Texas; 6. Ranger, Texas; 7. Burkburnett, Texas; 8. Desdemona, Texas; 9. Mexia, Texas; 10. East Texas, Texas; 11. El Dorado, Arkansas; 12. Smackover, Arkansas; 13. Louann, Arkansas; 14. Stephens, Arkansas; 15. Magnolia, Arkansas; 16. Jennings, Louisiana; 17. Caddo, Louisiana; 18. Naborton, Louisiana; 19. Zwolle, Louisiana; 20. Homer, Louisiana; 21. Haynesville, Louisiana; 22. Cotton Valley, Louisiana; 23. Tullos, Louisiana; 24. Rodessa, Louisiana; 25. Olla, Louisiana; 26. Red Fork, Oklahoma; 27. Cleveland, Oklahoma; 28. Glenpool, Oklahoma; 29. Cushing, Oklahoma; 30. Healdton, Oklahoma; 31. Osage, Oklahoma; 32. Tonkawa, Oklahoma; 33. Seminole, Oklahoma; 34. Oklahoma City, Oklahoma. (Drawing by Jon Gibson)

Fork (1901), Cleveland (1904), Glen Pool (1905), Cushing (1912), Healdton (1914), Osage (1920), Tonkawa (1921), Greater Seminole (1923), and Oklahoma City (1928) (Franks et al. 1981; Rister 1949).

So many people swarmed to the Cushing boom that its popup oil camps adopted the same suffix, much like using "ville" or "burg": Drumright, Dropright, Gasright, Alright, Deadright, Lastright, and Downright. Only Drumright survives. So much money followed in oil's wake that folks had trouble spending it. A report of the time showed that people bought new cars rather than fix flat tires (Franks et al. 1981, 58; Rister 1949, 202). One Osage Indian is said to have purchased ten cars in one year, while another is claimed to have bought a hearse and hired a chauffeur to drive him all over the country. An Osage woman reputedly spent $40,000 on a fur coat, diamond ring, new car, furniture, and Florida real estate—*all in a single day* (Franks et al. 1981, 58). So volatile were these booms (in this particular case, Ragtown, later Wirt) that the "most prosperous commercial establishment was the funeral home" (Franks et al. 1981, 126-27).

The combined output from these early fields made Oklahoma the national leader in crude oil production until surpassed by California in 1927 (Franks 1980), but the enormous flood of oil inundated the market, driving down the price to six bits a barrel. Fluctuating oil prices have always plagued the oil field. Producing more oil meant having to increase storage and delivery facilities. This enabled ever greater production, but the cycle had built-in roadblocks.

When more efficient rotary rigs replaced cable-tool rigs at the startup of Oklahoma's Tonkawa field, production rose dramatically, but oil prices fell commensurately (Franks et al. 1981, 4-5). The raging infernos—which destroyed so much oil and oil-field equipment at Cushing and Healdton during the "August Hell" of 1914 and the following year—actually doubled the price per barrel in 1916 and helped restore Oklahoma's profitability for more than a decade (Franks et al. 1981, 4).

Corsicana (1894) led Texas's discoveries, followed by the mighty Spindletop (1901) boom and nearby Saratoga (1901) and Sour Lake (1902) fields. Ranger (1917), Burkburnett (1918), Desdemona (1918), Mexia (1920), and numerous other plays around the state were rapidly brought in giving rise to the sentiment that "Texas floated on a sea of oil" (Weaver 1987, xi). In 1930, the extensive East Texas field around Kilgore was discovered (Olien and Olien 2002; Rister 1949; Rundell 1977). The East Texas field "marked the end of the gigantic early Texas oil booms" (Weaver 1987, vii).

Texas oil men promoted the replacement of cable-tool with rotary drilling, first with a fishtail bit and later with a rolling-cone bit, invented by Howard Hughes (Rundell 1977, 36, 81), and they pioneered the use of drilling mud, initially scooped out of cattle ponds, in order to bring drill cuttings to the surface and forestall well blowouts. They proved that salt domes trapped enormous reservoirs of oil, as Spindletop bore witness (Rundell 1977, 35-39). This legendary well rocked the oil community like Vesuvius did Pompeii, only without the casualties.

> Suddenly, the well disgorged vast quantities of mud with an explosive roar. The frightful noise continued as gas propelled upward. Then oil shot above the derrick too—the black plume doubling the derrick height, more oil gushing than any Texan had seen. More than anyone had ever seen, for the Lucas discovery well at Spindletop broke the world's record. In its first nine days, the well produced 800,000 barrels of oil. (Rundell 1977, 37)

Texas also issued the first production quotas and well-spacing regulations designed to slow rapid depletion of fields and stabilize prices (Rundell 1977, 226-27). These regulations helped because many of Texas's early fields are still producing over a hundred years later. Today, advances in technology—primarily horizontal drilling and fracking—have reenergized the oil industry. Gone are those old-time drillers who drove rigs by the sound of the spinning drill string and the feel of a hand brake. Brakes have now been replaced by joy sticks, as drillers monitor dials and gauges from the comfort of air-conditioned "dog houses" set up on location. Shouts of "Better take cover, boys, she's fixing to blow!" have become faint echoes from the past after blowout preventers were routinely installed on wells just before the Second World War. Ironically, modern company drillers often never see the oil they seek. In a 2015 conversation with the author, Gerald Brady stated that contract drillers normally do the fracking and complete the wells.

Southern Arkansas witnessed early strikes at El Dorado (1921) and Smackover (1922), at smaller adjoining plays of LouAnn and

Stephens, and later at Magnolia (1937). Unwanted saltwater and natural gas initially proved a problem (Franks and Lambert 1982, 107-109), but the enormous accompanying flow of crude quickly proved therapeutic. El Dorado's peak production came a year after discovery when over 10 million barrels were put in tanks, but Smackover was the titan, producing 69 million barrels at its peak in 1925 (Franks and Lambert 1982, 125). Yet, within a few years of discovery, these fields were rapidly depleted. Smackover was notorious for its careless waste of oil and gas.

> The field's huge flow of natural gas was generally burned off by giant torches or simply released into the air. . . . Smackover was "dotted with lakes of oil, lying at the mercy of the elements." During the summer, the dry weather often cracked the earthen dikes holding the crude and thus allowed it to seep onto nearby ground. Then, during the spring and winter months, heavy rains would wash out the restraining dirt and carry the crude into nearby creeks and bayous. . . . It was estimated that 2-8 percent of Smackover's oil production was wasted during the first twelve years of the field's life. . . . The waste of natural gas was even greater. One participant in the boom once counted twenty-five wells blowing wild at the same time in the field. (Franks and Lambert 1982, 126)

Just as the federal government was preparing to step-in, the state of Arkansas enacted legislation regulating the oil industry and shortly thereafter joined with neighboring oil-producing states to create the Interstate Oil Compact Commission (IOCC), which was established in order to stem waste and mitigate environmental degradation (Franks and Lambert 1982, 126).

Like El Dorado and many of the Texas strikes, Smackover was a boom town, a place where a rowdy male-dominated horde of humanity temporarily massed to exploit a quickly depleted pool of oil. Before oil was discovered, about sixty people called Smackover home. Three months later, population reached 5,000 and eventually peaked around 20,000 (Franks and Lambert 1982, 127). Lawlessness increased dramatically, and law enforcement agents came to be known as the Smackover Mounted Police because they patrolled the streets and alleys on horses.

The biggest problems, prostitution and gambling, centered in a collection of barrelhouses, called Death Valley. . . . There "oilfield doves" plied their trade openly during the night and rented horses at one dollar an hour during the day so they could ride among the drilling rigs selling their favors to the crews. Guns were carried openly, and fights were common. (Franks and Lambert 1982, 127)

Jennings (1901), located in the coastal prairies, led the procession in Louisiana, followed by finds in north Louisiana; among them: Caddo (1905), Naborton and Zwolle (1915), Homer (1919), Haynesville (1920), Cotton Valley (1925), Tullos-Urania (1925), Rodessa (1935), Olla (1940), and dozens of smaller plays (Franks and Lambert 1982).

Three years after Smackover, Tullos-Urania, too, experienced its own boom. Time, place, and personality notwithstanding, booms were embedded in the dynamics of early discovery and recovery. These first Arkansas ventures birthed two legendary figures who figured prominently at Tullos-Urania and Olla—speculator H. L. Hunt (Brown 1976; Hill 1994) and mule-skinner, later superb wildcatter, James Justiss (Justiss Oil Company 1996).

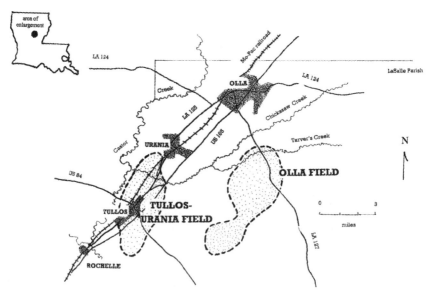

Tullos-Urania and Olla oil fields located in LaSalle Parish, Louisiana. (Drawing by Jon Gibson)

The frontispiece recalls Joe Hargrove's colorful characterization of mule-drawn oil-field wagons hauling supplies to drilling rigs through the deep mire that passed for roads in 1925. His and contemporaries' vivid recollections of the time and place set the historical stage for this book, which delves into the discovery and early development of the Tullos-Urania and Olla oil fields in LaSalle Parish, located in north Louisiana. These fields, only four straight-line miles apart, are not the earliest or richest fields in the four state region, but they are memorable because both are seen through the eyes of the hardhats who worked there and who participated in Tullos's nocturnal shenanigans.

No living soul has ever built a wooden derrick, run the brake on an old steam rig, or gee-hawed an eight-up mule team hauling a wagon load of pipe through Tullos gumbo. Those old timers have all "gone in the hole," as they say in the oil patch. We see their faces on faded photographs and hear their words on tape recordings.[1] In so far as possible, we rely on the old timers to tell this story. They lived it. Through their words, we vicariously share those old moments. Italicized quotes come directly from unedited taped conversations.

CHAPTER 1

Discovery Wells and Hardhats

Louisiana Piney Woods Oil Boom commemorates the discovery and subsequent recovery of oil in the Tullos-Urania and Olla fields in the piney woods of LaSalle Parish, located in northern Louisiana. Since the 1920s and continuing until this day, oil has been the prime mover of the area's economy, culture, and history. When first generation oil-field hands began to hang up their hardhats and trade their steel-toed boots for sneakers, their successors saw merit in recording old stories, bigger-than-life personalities, and an epic oral history that often outgunned the Wild West.

The book is based on interviews tape-recorded in 1983 by Juanita Fife Wall and in 1993 and 1994 by me. These recording sessions were not like academic question-and-answer interviews but were guided chats. Wall and I not only knew these celebrated characters, they were family and neighbors, albeit once removed. Tullos oil stained the soles of our shoes, just like theirs. We were all lulled to sleep by the staccato rhythm of the same pumpers and by the familiar aria of the shackle lines. Our fathers worked alongside these old hardhats, "pulling" the same old wells and "running" oil from the same old leases. I even "tailed tribbles" for a well on Tullos's N Lease. So, if the book waxes a bit familiar in places, you can blame it on my having grown up in Tullos.

Cameras were not common in oil-field tool boxes back then or now, but local residents managed to find a few faded pictures squirreled away in old family albums or in dusty, under-the-bed, shoe boxes. Other old pictures come from oil company archives. These rare gems give us a glimpse of life in the early Tullos-Urania and Olla oil fields.

H. Hardtner Huffman's retired hardhat. (Photograph by Jon Gibson, courtesy of Martha Fay Huffman Smith)

With camera in tow, I waded through mudholes and sawbriar patches looking for relics and ruins, a nostalgic search considering I grew up playing on these very same pieces of equipment when they were new and shiny. They were my toys and the oily spots where they sat, my private playgrounds. Ah, seems like only yesterday. I sought out memorable well locations with a hand-held GPS (via SONRIS coordinates), bent on photographing the old sites and anything remaining from their heyday. Initially, I wanted to pair vintage and contemporary photographs of the same locations in order to convey a sense of time passed, but old photographs proved as rare to come by as a silver dollar. Pine-shrouded derricks, rusty pumping units, rotten joints of pipe, stripped oil tanks, muddy lease roads, and other vestiges of the oil field were also photographically documented as I happened upon them in the overgrown barrens, as were surviving hand-tools of the trade, many curated in the private collection of driller Sonny King, who, for years, has been rescuing them from the elements.

Oil-stained ruins and discarded equipment used to be everywhere, but government-mandated cleanup and the sanitizing hand of nature are scrubbing the land. Today, little remains physically of the colorful history of these tumultuous times, and the hard-living souls who manned the rigs and patronized the bars during the boom days have all departed for heavenly bonanzas.

Crown block of old Urania Lumber Company derrick reaches above treetops on Chickasaw Creek along LA 125, near Urania, Louisiana, in spring of 1999. (Photograph by Jon Gibson)

Scabby pumper makes a living on the MWM Energy Miles Heirs lease in Tullos, Louisiana. (Photograph by Jon Gibson)

Going, going, gone – a rotted pipeline on M Lease. (Photograph by Jon Gibson)

Ribs showing, a plate-stripped lease tank hides in the pines near MWM Energy Miles No. 1 well. (Photograph by Jon Gibson)

Now graveled and passable, a Tullos Heirs lease road once bogged oil field wagons and mule teams. (Photograph by Michael Tradewell)

Thirty-six-inch pipe wrench in retirement on the King Drilling Company yard in Tullos, Louisiana. (Photograph by Carla Hallmark)

Louisiana Piney Woods Oil Boom is an ethnohistorical account of the early Tullos-Urania and Olla oil fields beginning with the wildcatting of the early 1920s and lasting for several decades afterwards. It is built around informant anecdote and participant observation. Among the informants were several old-timers who helped drill the discovery wells at Tullos-Urania and Olla, as well as many of the wells that followed, including W. C. "Willie" McDaniels, James "Jick" Justiss, and Joe Hargrove. The book reanimates their words, providing testimony to an age that no living soul can relate from direct experience—all eyewitnesses "have gone in the hole."

This book follows the trail of the wildcatters and relives the thrill of discovery (chapters 2-3). It retraces the march of gushers and rides out the Tullos boom days (chapters 4-5). It recounts Olla's strike and Urania's life on the edge of the boom (chapters 6-7). It puzzles over oil's origin and contemplates its underground home (chapter 8). In word and picture, early steam-powered drilling and pumping wells are rigged up, and oil is run from well to loading rack (chapters 9-11). Big-boy and poor-boy outfits once active in the fields are recalled (chapter 12) and finally the book touches on the social and economic impact of the boom and its aftermath (chapter 13).

Tullos-Urania and Olla strikes were like many early plays elsewhere in the midcontinent (Franks et al. 1981, 5-6; Rister 1949). First came discovery and leasing frenzy, followed by hordes of humans and fistfuls of dollars. After the rush came economic free-fall in places where fortunes were entirely oil-based or gradual decline in places where they were more diversified. Tullos-Urania and Olla differed from other boom towns in that the goings-on, characters, and personal relations were unique to time and place. Yet, the two fields were like night and day when it came down to the fervor of their respective strikes and the vitality of their recoveries.

Louisiana Piney Woods Oil Boom is not simply a history of people or events. The book is an account of early oil discoveries in north Louisiana as told through stories related by old-timers who actually participated in or witnessed the events.

CHAPTER 2
Wildcatting

Profitable quantities of oil were discovered in the Tullos-Urania field when Urania Petroleum Company's Urania Lumber Company No. 6 well blew out in March 1925. Nobody around today can say for sure why these early prospectors chose to "wildcat," or prospect, for oil in and around Tullos. Were they attracted by the nearby Castor Creek salt lick (E. Forrest Cook, pers. comm. 2010) — thought to be the cap of a salt dome (Huner 1939, 269-71)[1] — hoping that it was full of riches like Beaumont's Spindletop salt dome, one of the earliest and richest oil strikes in Texas (Rundell 1977, 35-39)? Tullos wildcatter Fred Stovall started his career at Spindletop, but he did not explore around the salt lick (Huner 1939, 270). His first Tullos wells were sunk several miles east of there (Fisk 1938, pl. 13). Were wildcatters lured because Tullos sits atop a topographic blister isolated by creek bottoms, suggesting that it might have been pushed upward by faulting or warping? Geologists knew that cracks or folds underground often trapped oil. Or was it the exposed Tertiary-age sediments and their fossils that caught the eye of these oil hunters? After all, it was a common belief that oil formed from the decomposed remains of these organisms, and it is reasonable to surmise that if their hard parts lay on the surface, then oil ought not to be far below.

Whatever drew them, these early wildcatters encountered shows of oil and gas as early as 1920 (Anonymous 1945, 4; Fisk 1938, 184; Franks and Lambert 1982, 75; Wall 1983, 5A). In the five years before No. 6 struck oil, ten or so wildcat wells were drilled and abandoned within the two township areas centered on Tullos — Township 10 North, Ranges 1-2 East (SONRIS 2000). According

Dead pine bakes in simmering heat of white flats of Castor Creek salt lick. (Drawing by Jon Gibson)

to James Elliott (1995, 22), Simms Oil Company drilled the first well in the Tullos-Urania field in 1920.[2] The well reached 3,500 feet, where it was pronounced dry. This may have been the Urania Lumber Company No. 1 (Serial No. 1963), which was permitted on December 19, 1919, and spudded (began drilling) on September 1, 1920 (SONRIS 2000). SONRIS gives no further details, but since the Urania Lumber Company No. 1 was the only well drilled that year in Section 8, Township 10 North, Range 2 East (Elliott 1995, 22), it is almost certainly the Simms well.[2]

One memorable wildcat was drilled by Fred Stovall in April 1924. The Louisiana Central Lumber Company No. 1 well (Serial No. 7723) was on Little Chickasaw Creek about two and a half miles slightly southeast of the location where the discovery well would be drilled nearly a year later. Stovall hit a gas pocket at 1,445 feet, and the well erupted, spewing a column of water and mud in a colossal release of 35,000,000 cubic feet of natural gas (Fisk 1938, 184). A gaping hole, 125 feet deep and half an acre wide, swallowed the drilling rig, boiler, and drill pipe (Wall 1983, 5A).

The event was recorded tongue-in-cheek by a Yale University student attending Henry Hardtner's nearby summer reforestation camp in 1924.

> April 6. An oil well in Section 27, south of the Chickasaw, struck gas and blew a mud geyser over the top of the derrick. At least 75,000,000 [*sic*] cubic feet of gas escaped in Urania and vicinity and all the fish in the Chickasaw (3 mud cats and 17 sunfish) were killed, while innumerable moccasins and turtles escaped overland on foot. . . . Most of the population of Louisiana visited the gusher by auto in the next few days and got stuck in the mud on the road by Bill Russell's residence. Somers and Shulley [Yale students] assisted one car out of a rut and the owners expressed deep regret that they could not give them a lift. A few yards further this car came to grief again and Somers *et al.* expressed equally serious concern at having to leave them there! (Anonymous 1924)

Joe Hargrove drove a mule team, worked in a bit shop, and roughnecked during Tullos's boom.[3] He recalled the first wildcat that actually brought oil to the surface. He couldn't remember the name of the well or the driller, but from his description, it probably was Stovall's Louisiana Central Lumber Company No. 2 (Serial No. 8070). It could not have been Stovall's nearby No. 1 well, because the ground engulfed that rig the year before, leaving no downhole pipe on which to hook a valve. Furthermore, Stovall was from Monroe — actually from the nearby town of Swartz. Louisiana Central Lumber Company No. 2 went to 2,033 feet and was capped in February 1925, just a month before the discovery well came in (SONRIS 2000).

The one [well] that first brought oil to the top of the ground, Frenchy

Robichaux [who later drilled the discovery well] was firing boilers on it. I can't think of the man's name — he was from Monroe but it wasn't Zeigen, he was an old wildcatter too [Fred Stovall is the person Hargrove is trying to remember]. And it was over there kinda out to the left of New Union Church back in there toward Little Chickasaw [Creek] in an old field. Well, they capped it off, and an old boy named Red [Mathews] — he worked there . . . was a watchman there — and there would be a big crowd come in there. . . . Saltwater and all would boil up there, you know, and bring this oil up, and he'd pass a hat around . . . and take up a collection. Then, he'd open the valve a little [and let] a little oil get in there a few seconds, and then he'd close it off right quick. Well, when another bunch would come in, he'd take up another collection, so he done pretty good. Well, they moved that rig over there where they put in the first discovery well, but actually that one was the one that had the first oil, oil coming to the top of the ground.

—Joe Hargrove, 1983

Tullos-Urania's shallow oil sands were not found at Olla. Oh, the Wilcox was there, all right, but its upper beds held no oil. One of the earliest Olla wildcats, Tremont Lumber Co. No. A-7 (Serial No. 9704), was spudded on May 28, 1925, just over two months after Tullos-Urania's No. 6 discovery well blackened the waters of Chickasaw Creek. Two weeks later, drilling was halted at 1,667 feet, the well pronounced dry, and the hole plugged (SONRIS 2000). Drilling proceeded sporadically in the two townships that would later comprise the heart of the Olla field, Townships 9-10 North, Range 2 East. Two more wildcats were drilled in 1925 and six in 1926, but then the search tailed off, only one each in 1927, 1930, and early 1931 (Fisk 1938, pl. 13), at which time drilling seems to have been suspended indefinitely — a baker's dozen without so much as putting a rainbow sheen in the mud pit.[4]

Tunica Petroleum Company was the busiest wildcatter in Tullos-Urania. Louisiana Oil & Refining Company was also active, and as many as nine other outfits were also looking for oil in the shallow Wilcox sands (Fisk 1938, pl. 13). Tunica Petroleum and Louisiana Oil & Refining also tried their luck at Olla, to no avail. Burban Oil and Gas, Dixie Oil, Gulf Refining, Hunt Oil, Minnesota Oil, Vacuum Oil, and a private interest or two joined them, but their holes were all duds, too (Elliott 1995, 22; Fisk 1938, pl. 13).

These wildcats showed that the top of the Wilcox formation at Olla was deeper than at Tullos-Urania, in some places more than

600 feet deeper. The average depth was 1,732 feet, with the deepest being 2,100 feet (Fisk 1938, pl. 13). Tullos-Urania oil pooled along the very top of the Wilcox between 1,500 and 1,550 feet down. Every one of Olla's wildcats went far below the upper boundary of the Wilcox. In Section 4, for instance, drillers dug eighty feet beneath the top of the Wilcox; in Section 27, they went 184 feet lower; in Section 13, 211 feet lower; in Section 22, 1,487 feet lower (Gulf Refining Co. Tremont Lumber Co. No. 1; Serial No. 14821); and in Section 10, a whopping 3,190 feet below the top of the Wilcox (Fisk 1938, pl. 13). Still, all came up empty—dry holes. It is easy to see why discouraged oilmen grew convinced that if they didn't strike oil at the top of the Wilcox, like at Tullos-Urania, there was no use cutting any deeper (Anonymous 1988, 8D; Baldwin et al. 2007, 14-15; Wall 1983, 5A).

A decade later, that old received wisdom proved unfounded. There was oil deeper in the Wilcox. It just hid much further down than anyone suspected. In Sections 4, 10, 13, 22, and 27, the average depth of the first ten producers was 2,750 feet (SONRIS 2000). The wildcats drilled in Sections 4, 13, and 27 stopped short of pay sand depth by 1,090 feet, 695 feet, and 1214 feet respectively. Yet, in Sections 10 and 22, the wildcats actually surpassed average pay sand depth by 2,169 feet and 245 feet respectively (SONRIS 2000), but those deep wells were bone dry too. In the drilling business, you can go by depth all you want to, but you better have your mojo working.

One thing was learned from the early dusters. If you were going to drill in the Olla area, you were going to have to go deep. H. L. Hunt did just that, and his mojo was working (Baldwin et al. 2007, 14-15). His mojo was named James Justiss.

In Tullos-Urania, oil hunters knew pay sand lay somewhere beneath their feet—Olla was another matter—but finding the mother pool was the big gamble. The El Dorado and Smackover (Arkansas) booms were winding down, and production in the Haynesville, Homer, and Caddo fields was flagging too (Franks and Lambert 1982; SONRIS 2000). Oil men were scrambling to find the next big strike. The stock market crash and the Great Depression were still four years away, plenty of time for fortunes to be made and lost, sometimes on the luck of the draw, the roll of the dice, or the click of a revolver hammer.

CHAPTER 3

The Day the Chickasaw Turned Black: The Discovery Well, Urania Petroleum Company's Urania Lumber Company No. 6

Discovery

The Urania Petroleum Company's Urania Lumber Company No. 6 (Serial No. 8488) was the discovery well for the Tullos-Urania field. It blew out in March 1925 from a depth of 1,512 feet in the top of the Wilcox sand (Fisk 1938, 184; SONRIS 2000).

> *We started to bail it, and it come in. We run a bailer in there three or four times . . . even set perforated pipe in the bottom of that well. . . . That's how come it to blow. I was right on the floor when it come in. I got wet. All of us got wet. . . . We didn't have nothing to cap it with. It was blowing open hole. We had no casing to cut in with . . . and so, it sanded up. We left it.*
> —W. C. McDaniels, 1994

The drilling rig was a fluid-circulating rotary rig, powered by two Lucy 72 steam boilers, according to McDaniels. The spudding drill was a twelve-and-a-half-inch fishtail bit. After cutting a few hundred feet, the bit was changed and a smaller drill was used to finish the well. The hole was made when Robichaux eased off the brake on the drawworks that turned the rotary causing the heavy drill string to spin and grind away the sands and clays below. The derrick was built of heavy pine lumber and stood crown-level with the surrounding pine trees. The location lay in a little bottom on the south bank of Chickasaw Creek between Tullos and Urania, just east of LA 125, which locals today call the "Old Road."

According to Joe Hargrove and W. C. McDaniels, No. 6 never produced marketable oil (Wall 1983, 5A). It flowed at a rate of about 800 to 1,000 barrels of clean oil per day in its hour lifetime (Fisk

The discovery well, Urania Lumber Company No. 6, and the drilling crew who brought it in on March 23, 1925. Left to right, O. "Frenchy" Robichaux was the driller, W. C. "Willie" McDaniels, Robert "Bob" Pendarvis, and an Ashworth worked the floor and fired the boilers, and a Williams boy was the derrickman. (Photograph by Jared, courtesy of W. C. McDaniels)

1938, 184), but sand choked off the well. The only oil recovered was what ran into nearby Chickasaw Creek, McDaniels noted in 1994. Attempts to clean out the well were unsuccessful, and it was abandoned. But that was enough. The discovery set off a drilling frenzy. The Tullos boom was on (Gibson 1999, 15-18; Wall 1983, 5A).

"The Well up on the Hill There that Pumped so Long"[1]

In May 1925, a little over a month after the discovery well sanded up, old wildcatter George Zeigen completed a direct offset to the discovery well, the Zeigen et al. Urania Lumber Company No. 1 (Serial No. 8639; SONRIS 2000), located about 400 yards west of No. 6 on the first high ground rising out of the Chickasaw floodplain. It struck oil at the top of the Wilcox sand at a depth of 1,512 feet (Fisk 1938, 184-85), the same depth as the discovery well. The oil came in

"And the well up on the hill there that pumped so long — that old walking beam [is still there] — that was George Zeigen's No. 1. That was the first well that produced commercially, you know." — Joe Hargrove, 1983. Visions of riches grip excited spectators watching the George Zeigen crew set casing. (Photograph by G. E. Johnson, courtesy of Tommy Sessions)

by heads, or in spurts of three to five barrels of two-minute duration at five-minute intervals for eleven hours, and then slowed to six-to-seven-barrel spurts every fifteen minutes for twelve more days (W. L. Holmes, quoted in Wall 1983; cf. Fisk 1938, 184). Joe Hargrove credits the Zeigen well with being "the first well that produced oil and put it in the line [pipeline]." In September 1925, four and a half months after completion, it was making seven barrels of oil a day (Fisk 1938, 185; Oil Weekly 1925, 67).

> *[There] was hundreds of [people] there, and Mr. Kinney, he was standing on the floor, and when it [the blowout] made that head up and come down, it come down on a lot of them there, he jumped up and said: "Whew! I'm a rich man."*
>
> —Joe Hargrove, 1983

Built of Oil

The serenity of the Chickasaw swamp ended that spring in 1925 with hissing steam engines and blowing oil. The sound of Robichaux and Zeigen's drilling rigs and others like them from Pennsylvania to California forever changed the face of America and the world. Although civil liberties were the lines political power-brokers drew in the sand when social conflicts arose, America's fortunes were built out of oil and her politics around the quest for it.

CHAPTER 4

The March Toward Pendarvis Prairie

During the remainder of 1925, forty wells were permitted in the two townships around Tullos (SONRIS 2000). Exploration steadily marched south out of the big, old-growth woods along Little Chickasaw Creek and onto the grassy cone flower-appointed Pendarvis Prairie around downtown Tullos.

In January 1926, Arkansas oilman H. L. Hunt, entered the frenzy by acquiring the Tullos Heirs lease, an eighty-eight-and-a-half-acre tract lying between the Missouri-Pacific railroad and Castor Creek (Robert Gray, William Davis, and Delbert Noble, pers. comm. 1983).

Cone flowers bask in the summer sun on Tullos Heirs lease near Tullos depot. (Photograph by Jon Gibson)

He paid $32,000 for this acreage, a decidedly risky investment because Standard Oil of New Jersey had stopped buying Tullos crude after it was deemed unsuitable as fuel oil (Wall 1983, 5A). Hunt tells of the venture:

> I proceeded to get a lease and started drilling. The Hunt "luck" came through again and I brought in a well, which produced crude with a high lube content, but asphalt base, and was not very popular. There was no market for this oil and it looked like a bad situation for getting any money out of it. I was making about 400 barrels a day from this shallow well. I was always fond of shallow production. (Hunt 1973; quoted by Robert Gray, William Davis, and Delbert Noble, pers. comm. 1983)

By summer, Hunt had drilled a dozen shallow wells on the lease, none deeper than 1,519 feet and all but one of them, producers (Robert Gray, William Davis, and Delbert Noble, pers. comm. 1983; SONRIS 2000; Wall 1983, 5A). During the first year, the lease produced approximately 1,700 barrels of oil per day (Robert Gray, William Davis, and Delbert Noble, pers. comm. 1983).

Tullos Heirs lease road leading to tank uphill. (Photograph by Jon Gibson)

Now, I helped drill old 10 [Serial No. 9553], 9 [Serial No. 9552], and 3 [Serial No. 9425]. . . . When I left down there [retired, c. early 1960s], I believe it was ten wells running. They had a big power down there pulling them . . . for years, and it got too expensive, so they shut it down and put pumping rigs on all of them. Some of them still had them old standard rigs on them . . . Tullos Heirs 10 and 6 [Serial No. 9549], I believe, still had a . . . rig on it, standard rig, big old bullwheel.

—W. C. McDaniels, 1994

Remarkably, seven of those Tullos Heirs wells were still producing in 2010, more than eighty years after they were drilled. These eternal pumpers include No. 3., No. A-12 (Serial No. 9427), No. A-13 (Serial No. 9428), No. 7 (Serial No. 9550), No. 10 (Serial No. 9553), No. A-14 (Serial No. 9574), and No. 13 (Serial No. 9883) (SONRIS 2000). Nos. 6 and A-11 have been converted to saltwater disposal wells, and No. 15, permitted on July 15, 1926, was never drilled (SONRIS 2000). The other five have been abandoned.

Within a year after the discovery well came in, from March 25, 1925, to March 25, 1926, 200 well permits were issued for the two

Last of its kind, the big, old bandwheel along US Highway 84 near junction with US Highway 165. (Photograph by Jon Gibson)

*This shallow well was the H. L. Hunt, Inc. Tullos Heirs No. A-11 Serial No. 9314,
which was initially referred to as No. 1. (Anonymous 1945; SONRIS 2000). It was
the first well Hunt drilled on the Tullos Heirs lease. It came in on February 16, 1926,
flowing at an initial rate of 700 barrels a day. Production came from eight feet of sand
between 1,482 feet and 1,490 feet in the top of the Wilcox (Anonymous 1945; Wall
1983, 5A). As recently as summer 2015, it held the distinction of being the oldest
continually producing well in Tullos (SONRIS 2000). (Photograph by Jon Gibson)*

townships alone. The next year, March 26, 1926, to March 26, 1927,
245 wells were permitted in the same two townships. Not all were
producers, but most were, and during the two-year span of 1926-
27, the Tullos-Urania field produced more than 7,500,000 barrels of
oil, or an average of around 10,400 barrels per day (Fisk 1938, 187-
188; Shaw 1933). Production peaked in June 1926 at 19,400 barrels
per day (Teas 1927, 683).

Big well after big well was brought in during those two years
when the field was new and full of gas. The Natural Gas and Fuel
Oil Corporation brought in one of the most dramatic, the Tullos
No. 3 (Serial No. 9178), a gusher that blew out around the first of
February 1926. Located near the old depot just south of the present-
day Baptist church, the well shot crude over the derrick crown at
the rate of about 2,500 barrels of clean oil and 3,000,000 cubic feet of
gas per day (Fisk 1938, 185). Harold Fisk says the release came from
four feet of sand at a total depth of 1,548 feet. After a day, the well

stopped flowing. Reworking restored the flow but only for another ten hours (Fisk 1938, 186).

Tullos barely had time to recover from the excitement of the Tullos No. 3 well before another gusher showered Main Street with crude. The Goodwin and Daniels Hardy Tullos No. 1 (Serial No. 9233), located behind (east of) the present-day post office in old downtown Tullos, blew out on February 6, 1926, sending a huge column of oil and sand skyward.

Fisk (1938, 186) describes the well as having an:

> Initial flow of 1,000 barrels per day from a total depth of 1,552 feet. It was reported that the well later increased to around 7,500 barrels per day, if allowed to flow open. However, although it was making clean oil, it blew out several tons of sand and was, therefore, closed in at night so that it was actually making 3,500 barrels per day. (Fisk 1938, 186)

W. C. McDaniels, who worked on the discovery well, recalls the Goodwin and Daniels well:

Long-ago Tullos calm before the excitement in spring of 1926. Old No. 3 is the well on the left. (Photograph by S. G. Wilson, courtesy of Lorraine Byrd and Luther Byrd)

[The Daniels well] made about 10,000 barrels [sic] a day there. Two times! It done it for a long time, then quit, and they went back in to try to put tubing in to pump it, you know, and that thing blowed in again. Dang, it made oil, pure oil. . . . They had pumps sitting on that road that goes across there to the other [East Herbert Street between LA 125 and US Highway 165], down there in that flat. They . . . had a levee across, and they had pumps sitting all in there picking that oil up because it was running wild. It was seven inch casing, and it just kept blowing out. . . . It was blowing all time.

— W. C. McDaniels, 1994 (Gibson 1999, 44)

The well was high drama.

I believe it was later then [than the Hardtner-Edenborn & Collins No. 2] – it might have been before that time – than that one [the Goodwin and Daniels well][1] back of the schoolhouse there at Tullos blew out, and, aw, it was blowing, and it kind of cratered a little bit, and your dad [M. W. Fife Sr.] went in there with his teams and hooked onto that stuff and pulled it out . . . , and that . . . sand was scattered – that white saltwater sand – all over the trees and everything and looked like a heavy snow. So, he got it all out though. He told me he'd get it all out, and he did. He got it all out.

— Joe Hargrove, 1983

In a 1983 interview with Joe Hargrove, Juanita Fife Wall, Fife's daughter, recalls her daddy being paid $500, big bucks for a job so dangerous that just one spark could have touched off a fireball that would have burned down the whole town.

February's skein of making spectacular wells continued into 1927. On February 21, 1927, Louisiana Oil & Refining Corporation brought in the Tremont Lumber Company No. B-17 (Serial No. 9273). Located about a half mile north of the US 165-US 84 intersection and a few hundred yards west of US 165, the well struck pay sand at a total depth of 1,536 feet (SONRIS 2000). It blew out making 1,800 barrels of crude a day and was still flowing at that rate more than a week later (Fisk 1938, 186).

Another exciting blowout happened on November 19, 1928, near Castor Creek, west-northwest of the commissary in Urania. The Hardtner-Edenborn & Collins No. 2 (Serial No. 12276) struck gas at 690 feet and shot a plume of gas and sand into the air with a deafening roar. The omnipresent Joe Hargrove was also involved with this well:

Winberry was running the rig, and it blew out, and, oh, it was roaring. We could hear it clean up there, [where] we lived in a big old house . . . right close to where the lease was. Well, news [come] that they'd capped some of them wild wells in Arkansas. So, we'd take this crew — and I was one of them — and we'd cap the well the next morning. Oh, we was dreading it, hoping it'd sand over or something. So, sure enough, next morning we didn't hear it, but we went over there, and the whole well was just covered with sand. It didn't crater — it did have a crater close there — but this one didn't crater.

—Joe Hargrove, 1983

The Hardtner-Edenborn & Collins blowout site was a local attraction for years.

The casing head (and I assume still does) leaks a small amount of natural gas and has for as long as I can remember and usually had a small flame burning. Enough that at times a hobo or maybe more than one had erected a small shack over the wellhead and used the flame for cooking and I suppose in cold weather, as a heating source.

—E. Forrest Cook, 2010

The march toward Pendarvis Prairie and on south toward Rochelle proved the Tullos-Urania producing zone lay within a three to four mile radius of downtown Tullos, and Tullos in 1926 had a rough-and-rowdy downtown, which ran a half-mile north-south and wide open day-and-night. By the end of 1926, a year and nine months after Urania Lumber Company No. 6 struck oil, 360 wells had been drilled in the Tullos-Urania field. Although only around 20 percent were making more oil than saltwater, the maximum daily oil production still reached nearly 20,000 barrels (Teas 1927, 683). The boom was on.

CHAPTER 5
"Man, It Was Terrible":[1]
Tullos Boom Days

Word of Robichaux's strike spread like a blowout, and within days, a writhing mass of humanity descended on Tullos. A tent town sprang up on a hill near the discovery well. Tents were pitched *"in every place big enough to stretch one"* (W. C. McDaniels, pers. comm. 1994). Over the next several months, drilling shifted southward, followed by scores of one-room shacks along the main road (Doughty 1974, 18). Boardinghouses crowded Tullos's main street. Made of red-heart pine with tarpaper roofs, these windowless buildings had a lobby in front and a long, narrow hall running all the way to the back with eight to ten small rooms lining each side of the hall (Baldwin et al. 2007, 14; Doughty 1974, 13; Anonymous 1988, 8D). In summer, vagrants slept under the stars in broom sage fields and in winter, inside the warm belt halls of the standard rigs. Hijackings grew so common around the rigs that lease pumpers started burning off the tall grass where robbers lay in ambush (M. W. Fife Jr., pers. comm. 1994). "No-gooders" also perched up in the rafters of the belt halls, ready to pounce on unsuspecting pumpers, bushwhacking and sometimes even killing them.

Main Street

Some estimates put Tullos's population as high as 10,000, mostly men (Doughty 1974, 13), but on any given day, there probably were never more than a few thousand people manning and supplying the rigs, running the cafés and bars, and loitering on the streets (Claude Gibson, pers. comm. 1994; Gibson 1999, 16). A shadow population came out in droves after dusk, adding gambling, bootlegging,

39

hijacking, prostitution, and even murdering to Tullos's thriving vocations. But natives—the few hundred souls who were born and raised on Castor Creek, especially women folk—stayed out of town or else dashed in and out of town on weekends for staples and church services, always during daylight. The hubbub was a remarkable transformation for this quiet farming and logging community, whose only previous brush with such a transient invasion came thirty years before with the building of the railroad in the early 1890s (Anonymous n.d., 10; Elliott 1995, 6-8).

> *Coming on in Tullos, there was nine of those houses, if I remember right. Every one of them stuffed full of pretty gals, and, Lord, the mud — it was hub deep to the wagon and belly deep to the mules — so we come through there hauling, and it'd [the wagon] almost bog down. And they hollered: "Hey, buddy, come on in here. . . . Come up."*
>
> —Joe Hargrove, 1983

The fledgling town is ramped up with activity. Twelve wells are visible, three derricks under construction, one being drilled (the drill string connected to the traveling block), and others waiting to be drilled, already producing, or abandoned. Some of the older gable and ell houses are being torn down to make room for new boardinghouses. At least three boardinghouses line Main Street: one being built,[2] an occupied one across the street, and another occupied one at the lower end of town. There are several large buildings with front galleries and long halls in the back that are probably hotels, and there is an older two-story hotel back up the street toward Urania, possibly dating from the time of railroad construction three decades earlier. One-room shacks are crammed into every nook and cranny. The old First Baptist Church, which doubles as the school during the week, sits on the lower end of town. In the center of town is George Tullos's general store, which is doing a good business judging by the number of T-Models parked around it. A few tired mules await marching orders down at the depot, a make-do affair comprised of two railroad boxcars, and a yoke of oxen is getting ready to deliver a steam boiler to a rig. A mule-drawn eight-up, low-wheel oil wagon is hauling a load of pipe or lumber toward a new well location marked by a stack of heavy timbers. Oil wagons line the fence behind Tullos's store. H. L. Hunt's loading rack is operating, and high water covers Louis Tullos's bottom field next to Castor Creek.

Wooden derricks being constructed along Tullos's main street during the boom in spring of 1926. Photo taken from the crown of a derrick behind the Orrin Capps grocery store. (Photograph by S. G. Wilson, courtesy of Lorraine Byrd and Luther Byrd, Tullos.)

George Tullos's store draws Coca-Cola drinking crowd along the town's main street during the boom in spring of 1926. Photo taken from the crown of a derrick behind the Orrin Capps grocery store. (Photograph by S. G. Wilson, courtesy of Lorraine Byrd and Luther Byrd)

Tullos during the boom was a rip-roaring, shoot-'em-up kind of place, where leases were won in poker games, deals sealed with a handshake, and arguments settled in shootouts. Lots of money rode into town in Ford's Tin Lizzies and lots, lots more rode out in T&GY tankers cars. And on Sunday, Tullos rested and souls were saved at Tullos First Baptist Church, photographed here in 1926. (Courtesy of Ferndale McKeithen, Centennial Cultural Center)

A Rip-Roaring, Shoot-'Em-Up Kind of Place

Ellis "Red" Doughty, who was town marshal from 1930 to 1936, writes:

> Crime was rampant, illegal sale of liquor, gambling of all kinds, poker, craps, roulette, shell games, confidence men, and all other means to separate a man from his money, were wide open. Illegal sale of drugs were prevalent. Hijacking occurred nearby every night and some were known to have taken place in daylight. It was not unusual for a man to be slugged, his money and other valuables taken from him, and left unconscious. Many of them died without anyone ever knowing the circumstances of their death. (Doughty 1974, 13)

And:

> I learned . . . that fist fights, some gang fights were almost a daily occurrence and knife and gunfights were not unusual. I was

an eyewitness to four killings. Three of these were close enough to me that I could have put my hands on the victims as they fell. One was slashed across the throat, severing his jugular vein. Two others were shot and died instantly. One, I am sorry to say, was a victim of my own gun after he stabbed me three times with an ice pick and continued to try to stab me. (Doughty 1974, 14)

In 1934, Clara Belle Evans and her husband Sam moved to Tullos to run a grocery store on the main street. Clara Belle was one tough lady. Many times, I saw her carry a 100-pound sack of feed on her shoulder and another on her outthrust hip. Why, on one occasion, she even stuffed the intestines back into a bus-chasing dog and sewed up the wounded canine with needle and thread. The dog lived to chase one more bus! Clara Belle told me about her trepidation in leaving the relative safety of the nearby lumber-mill towns of Midway and Georgetown for the wild streets of Tullos:

> *The first time I ever saw Tullos is when we moved here. I'd never been here because they were killing people, you know, every week they'd kill a man . . . and the law was the one that killed them mostly.*
> —Clara Belle Evans, 1994 (Gibson 1999, 17)

Joe Hargrove remembered several killings.

Sam and Clara Belle Evans' grocery store, downtown Tullos, c. 1945. Left to Right: an unidentified woman with her back to the camera, Sam Evans, Clara Belle Evans, Claude Gibson, and an unidentified man. (Courtesy of Rene Evans Lurry)

There was a restaurant there owned by a Greek. Once when we were eating dinner and a fellow we called Peg because of his peg-leg came in. He had been drinking. He bought something . . . and claimed he had paid for it. The Greek said he hadn't, and when Peg went after the Greek behind the counter the Greek shot and killed him. They put the Greek in the pen for three years but it was self-defense.

—Joe Hargrove, 1983 (Williams 1976, 6)

Gambling was a deadly pastime too. Again, Joe Hargrove:

There was a fellow . . . called him Slim. . . . He liked to gamble when he got paid, Saturday night. So we was in there gambling, and there was three card-sharks, outlaws — one named Williams, another they called Blackie . . . and another, I forget what his name was. Well, they was taking [Slim] for a cleaning pretty quick, so old Slim just raised up with a fan-style forty-five and shot all three of them down and thought he'd killed them, emptied his gun. But as he started out the door, Williams got his gun and shot him in the back and killed him. . . . About a week or two later, well they found a black man down in that hollow, got a stray bullet, was probably there trying to bootleg.

—Joe Hargrove, 1983

And, of course, drinking aided and abetted the wildness, the law notwithstanding.

During the height of the boom, we had a sheriff, name of McDowell. Well, there was a fellow . . . he was drinking up in this up-story building, raising sand.[3] And he [McDowell] went up there to get it straightened out . . . and they got into it. The story was told that he [McDowell] tried to hit the fellow over the head with a pistol, and he [the drunk] shot him and killed him. Well, he [the drunk] come down, and there was one by the name of Red Bailey and another one they called Cowboy — he wore a big cowboy hat — and two or three more shooting at him [the drunk]. Well, they run across the street in the end hotel where Felix Long had a barbershop, and they shot him [the drunk] through and through six times, and he [the drunk] shot Red Bailey, one of his fingers off. They handcuffed him. . . . Chief of police [marshal], name of Bradford, he came in and made them take the handcuffs off of him. Sent him to the hospital, and he got alright.

—Joe Hargrove, 1983

After the McDowell shooting, town marshal Bradford was involved in another fatal shooting—his own.

[Shorty] had a nice-looking wife, fine lady seemed like, and [Bradford] made advances toward her, and, so, one day this husband of hers [Shorty] come in and killed him. So, they put him in jail, but he come clear and they got him out of town. And they say, a year or two later that some of [Bradford's] boys found him in East Texas, and they killed him.

— Joe Hargrove, 1983 (Williams 1976, 6)

Guns facilitated the bootlegging business in the old days too.

There was a big fellow — I forget his name but [he] ran a pool hall right across from . . . the bank . . . , and he was a bootlegger but he was mean. Said he'd killed several men. I don't know whether he had or not . . . and [he] fell in with a young fellow by the name of Busby. And he [Busby] was bootlegging on the outside and was kinda getting some of Big One's trade, and they got in an argument. [Big One] told him not to come around his place, so he [Busby] went back to the place where he was rooming and got his gun and come [back and killed Big One].

— Joe Hargrove, 1983

High Yo, Silver, Away. Tullos's very own Lone Ranger, marshal Vic Loflin, who succeeded Bradford, carried silver bullets and a night stick but left his gun at home. Loflin was marshal from 1936 into the 1950s. (Photograph by Carla Hallmark)

After the frenzy of the boom subsided in the late 1930s, Tullos began to resemble a normal town, at least before dusk settled. Downtown stayed busy five days a week, but some establishments took no time off. Downtown was only a block long, but the main street (LA 125) was lined with businesses. Heading north from the telephone switchboard office (run by Mrs. Benson) along the left (west) side of the street were Linny Adam and Pan Weaver's rooming house; Phil Gaharan's doctor's office; a vacant lot where traveling carnivals put up their booths and rides; Sam and Clara Belle Evans' grocery and feed store; Steve Chevalier's (subsequently Bamburg's and later Dewitt and Billie Roshtos') café and upstairs "boarding" house; Felix Long's barber shop; Jim Gibson's fish market; Monroe Masters's café and bar; Aaron Ashley's Western Auto; Pinkie's Bar; Willard Martin's (later Shaw's) barber shop; and Nugent's (later McManaman's; Lee Norsworthy's; and, subsequently, Jitney Jungle) grocery.

Turning around here and heading back through town (on the east side of Main Street), you passed Jack Jarvis's bar and pool hall; Hardtner Huffman's hardware; Huffman's lumber storage; Hazel Martin's clothing store; Ott Milam's drug store; Coffeepot Café; Jimmy Bardin's bar and pool hall; Herbert Russell's dry goods; Cockerham's (later Hobson's) five and dime; J. W. and Orrin Capps' grocery; Gammill's appliance store; the Princess movie theater and Brown Derby (a coffee and ice-cream shop); and several vacant lots before reaching the post office, run by Becky Dunlap and Carrie Doughty. Next to the post office was the town hall and jail, and just beyond sat the old wooden First Baptist Church, which also served as the first grammar school and later as Milam's Furniture store. The church and the school moved to the other (north) end of' downtown after separate new brick buildings were constructed in the late 1940s. Luther Dunn's machine shop was next door to the old church. The last place of business on the east side of the road was Harold Williams's motor company and body-and-paint shop, about a quarter-mile below the machine shop.

Above downtown, on the right hand side of the road going north toward Urania, you went by the new grammar school (after 1948); the LaSalle State Bank; Martin's dry goods (old store); another ice cream parlor; Placid's warehouse; the Methodist church; and Bud Shufflin's saloon and gas station at the US 84 intersection.

Saturday thrills, the Princess theater circa 1930s where Hopalong Cassidy shot six-shooters out of villains' hands on the silver screen and Lash LaRue, in person, thrilled youngsters with his cracking whip. (Courtesy of Lane Capps and Myrtle Pendarvis Mellichamp)

Headed back toward downtown on the opposite side of the road, you passed Johnnie Maxwell's waco and magneto repair shop; Herbert DePriest's (later Charley Wiggins's) Cities Service station; Ed Gammill's Selma Motor Company; Lessye Brown's café; Stella Henslee's café (later, Selma Motor Company's car showroom); a two-lane bowling alley; a skating rink; a jewelry shop; Shelton's café; Homer Girod's service station; McMillan's grocery store (later, a rent house and, subsequently, an educational building for the church), and, after 1946, the new brick First Baptist Church. Next came the road to the depot, and then you were back at Norsworthy's beauty shop.

Several more establishments — Shep Haynes's bar; Amos Moore's bar and "rent" houses; Billie Roshto's bar and "boarding" house; Doodle White's bar; Van Dunlap's bar; and Frank and Lucy Allen's bar — competed for patrons along US 84. Jimmy Morrison's general

In 1941 pretty carhop Kathren Maxwell was responsible for taking orders at Lessye's Café in Tullos. (Courtesy of Jon Gibson family collection)

store, gas station, and motel, as well as oil-field supply companies, also fronted the highway.

The town was also patronized by Bonnie Parker and Clyde Barrow, the infamous murderers, robbers, and kidnappers. Their crime spree ended in a hail of bullets along a lonely stretch of backroad between Gibsland and Sailes in Bienville Parish in 1934 (Guinn 2010).

> Bonnie Parker and Clyde Barrow visited Chevalier's Café shortly before their visit to an ambush. My mother, her sister, my Aunt Ora, and Aunt Ora's small daughter Marie were in the café eating while Bonnie and Clyde were eating. Marie . . . had a snotty nose and was roaming around the room.
> Bonnie said, "Come here, baby, and let me wipe your nose."
> She took a napkin and wiped Marie's nose. Mother and Aunt Ora talked about that often.
> —John Lee Doughty, Jr., 2010

Tullos mayor Felix Long and a friend, Hosey Coleman, were also in the café at the time. W. F. Long, Felix's son, shared their view of the events with Doughty.

Felix was at a table drinking coffee with Hosey Coleman.

Hosey whispered, "Felix, that's Bonnie and Clyde at that table. What are you going to do about it?"

Felix said, "Not a [expletive deleted] thing. Look out the front door."

Just outside the front door was parked the Ford Clyde loved so much, parked sideways, driver's side to the door. In the driver's seat was a woman. She was positioned so she could keep her eyes on Bonnie and Clyde and the other people in the café. Poking above the door window-frame was the barrel of a sub-machine gun. So, Bonnie and Clyde ate peacefully and left Tullos.

—John Lee Doughty, Jr., 2010

Another celebrity patronized one of Tullos's drinking parlors. Doughty (1996) relates the event. Hank Williams stopped off at Amos Moore's bar during one of his road tours. After playing "Your Cheatin' Heart" for the thrilled patrons, Hank asked them if they wanted to hear him play the song backwards. Amid thunderous clapping, Hank turned around on his stool and played it again.

Years later, Tullos was still a fount of the amber liquid. Doughty recalls the daily bustle around just one of the dozen or so beer joints in 1959.

A friend and classmate, Mike White, . . . at the ripe old age of seventeen, inherited a bar in Tullos. Black bootleggers from dry Jena, ten times the size of Tullos and sixteen miles away, and dry Winnfield, twenty times the size of Tullos and twenty miles away, met beer delivery trucks in my friend's parking lot. . . . Several hundred thousand cases of beer left that parking lot and several million dollars passed over the counter. . . . Since the 1920s there has been an oil well or two—or even three—in every vacant lot in Tullos, but far more barrels of beer have passed through Tullos than barrels of oil pumped from beneath Tullos. (Doughty 1996)

But Tullos, Olla, and Urania were not completely, or even mostly, distilled from bad mash, although Tullos during the boom had more than its fair share. A subtle disconnect ran through these towns, one so subliminal that factions rarely were aware of their counterparts. Families, schools, and churches created stable community (Plummer 1963, 1; Caraway 1979, 10D). Card playing, drinking, hijacking, and killing did not. Still, unless violence spilled onto the street from the bars or a church deacon happened to be seen going into the back door of a beer joint, the "good" and "bad" factions usually ignored each other.

Schoolgirl Daphne McLeod remembers a calmed-down Tullos during the mid-1950s:

> Tullos had the dubious distinction of having 3 churches and 13 beer joints. It was the only wet town in LaSalle [P]arish, and men came from miles around to partake of its liquors. . . . I didn't understand booze and drinking and being drunk, and all this scared me quite a lot. But it didn't make me unhappy. It was just a part of Tullos.
> —Daphne McLeod, 1998 (Gibson 1999, 17)

Only rarely did the two sides engage in open conflict. Over a two-week period in February 1935, the Tullos First Baptist Church sought to purge the congregation of members who failed to live up to the church covenant, which included prohibitions against drinking and fornication (Mott 1935). Twenty-nine members were publicly charged with misconduct—several admitted guilt, asked for forgiveness, and had their membership reinstated. One unrepentant soul publically bade the church to exclude him from their fellowship, and twelve others were stricken from the church rolls, *in absentia*. Six months later, the preacher resigned (Mott 1935).

Forty years later in 1976, the conflict surfaced again. The church spearheaded a call for a local election for the purpose of getting rid of alcohol sales in town.

> Tullos's four hundred mostly god-fearing souls stepped in the voting booth, pulled the curtain closed, and, then, with only the eyes of God watching and not the eyes of preachers, voted like they wanted. They kept beer in Tullos and voted in whisky. (Doughty 1996)

Boom, Boom, Boom, Boom

What made Tullos unlike Olla and other nearby towns was that it sat squarely in the middle of the oil field. Derricks and tanks rose above house tops, oil branches flowed through yards, and pumping wells and shrieking shackle lines provided continual racket all over town. One downtown café used an abandoned well's open casinghead as a toilet. Roughnecks, roustabouts, and pumpers clamored about in their noisy trucks, always going to or coming from some drilling location, broken well, or tank battery. For Tullos natives, the sights, sounds, and smells of the oil field were as taken for granted as eating mama's fried chicken on Sundays. Yet, when five o'clock came, Tullos's day was only half done. Family men went home to supper. Others flocked to beer joints, joined by a daily wave of out-of-towners, as the town revved up for its nocturnal activities.

And so it was.

CHAPTER 6
Olla Field

The breakout well in Olla was the H. L. Hunt Goodpine Oil Company No. 1 (Serial No. 23496), located in the pines north of LA 127 and Little Chickasaw Church. Spudded on December 18, 1939, it blew out just before Christmas, but it showed Hunt what he was looking for — deep Wilcox oil and gas. Hunt called in James "Jick" Justiss, his general superintendent, who was then working in Cotton Valley, Louisiana, to repair the well (Anonymous 1996 a, 3). Knowing he already had pay sand in hand, Justiss sent the well down to 8,997 feet in search of even deepest plays. He found none. By April 22, 1940, he had the well back on line, making oil from five feet of sand between 2,267 and 2,272 feet (SONRIS 2000). That five feet of sand produced for eighteen years until the well was plugged and abandoned on February 26, 1958.

Although Goodpine Oil Company No. 1 was the first Olla well to strike oil and gas (Anonymous 1996a, 3), it was not the discovery well for the Olla field. That distinction belonged to Hunt's WX D RA SU76 Louisiana Central Oil and Gas No. 9 (Serial No. 23782), a companion well drilled a few hundred yards south of the Goodpine No. 1 well when No. 9 was being deepened (Baldwin et al. 2007, 3). Spudded on February 15, 1940, No. 9 came in on February 26, 1940. It reached 2,983 feet, but production came from four feet of sand between 2,270 and 2,274 feet (SONRIS 2000). Not only is No. 9 the discovery well, but it is the oldest continually producing well in the Olla field. Just how much oil the well was making in the early days is anybody's guess, but we do know it was making more than 62,000 barrels a month up until January 1977. It took five more years before production slipped below 30,000 barrels a

Goodpine Oil Company No. 1 location. An open mud pit is all that remains at this pine-reclaimed location. (Photograph by Jon Gibson)

month for the first time in March of 1983, and it was still making 770 barrels of oil a month in the spring of 2010 (SONRIS 2000), seventy years after it was brought in. Just think, if Hunt had been getting today's dollars [$45/bbl] for January's 1977 oil, he would have been pulling in $2,790,000 a month from just one well, but at the time, oil was selling for around a paltry dollar and a half per barrel, barely enough to keep Hunt's name on the Forbes list. Even at today's reduced flow, old No. 9 is still earning its keep, nearly $35,000 dollars a month.

According to W. C. McDaniels (pers. comm. 1994), Hunt was playing the horses at a Florida racetrack when the discovery well was completed, *"and they just shut down [the well] 'til he come in."* He returned to Olla for the staged valve-opening ceremony, all gussied up in a dark buttoned-up suit with bow-tie and dress shoes — the wealthy oilman personified. Oilfield dignitaries and Olla merchants converged on the wellhead to pay homage.

Within a year, 110 wells were drilled at Olla (SONRIS 2000), and H. L. Hunt Inc. (later Placid Oil Company) led the charge with

Sporting a fresh coat of paint, Olla's discovery well, Hunt's Louisiana Central Oil and Gas No. 9, still makes barrels of oil and bales of money. (Photograph by Jon Gibson)

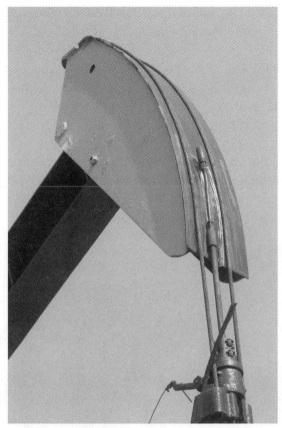

Old No. 9 lifts crude from 2,270 feet below.
(Photograph by Jon Gibson)

James Justiss calling the shots, followed closely by Arkansas Fuel Oil Company. The next year (between February 27, 1941, and February 27, 1942), 132 wells were permitted; the following year (February 28, 1942, to March 1, 1943), there were 103 permitted wells; and thereafter one well in each of the next two years (until March 2, 1945) (SONRIS 2000). Olla has over 1,200 wells today, and just under a third are still producing (SONRIS 2000).

Fifteen years makes a lot of difference in the oil field, and, unlike Tullos-Urania's wells, most of Olla's were brought in peacefully, under control. Technology made the biggest difference, especially the blowout preventer, or BOP—an assembly of high-pressure valves designed to reduce gas pressure coming up the drill hole from the formation. Lacking BOPs, early Tullos wells often came in like a pricked balloon, shooting water, oil, and sand out of the drill pipe as natural gas trapped for eons in the formation rocketed to the surface. Even though Olla's deeper oil sands held much more gas than Tullos-Urania's, BOPs lessened the likelihood of blowouts, sanding-in, and catastrophic cratering. In addition, well makers became more proficient at detecting porous oil-bearing sands before they punched into them, thereby reducing the risk of violent gas releases in the first place. Electric logging ("slumberjaying" after Schlumberger, the name of the logging company), seismic surveying (shooting the well), precision coring, and heavier drilling mud replaced the guesswork, taste tests, and barefoot muck of earlier days.

Black rain from down below. Penrod gusher in Olla field, July 3, 1940. (Courtesy of Jennifer Loe and Justiss Oil Company)

Telling which strata were most likely to host oil and gas was enabled by logging—measuring stratigraphic resistance to an electrical current run down the well's borehole (electric logging) or measuring stratigraphic response to a shock wave generated by a small explosion set off in a small hole drilled near the well (seismic surveying). These tests revealed differences in "rock" density, or porosity. Oil-bearing sands were porous, and well makers poured over the resulting depth-graduated graph looking for porous strata.

A lot was riding on these logs. Max W. Maxwell, a small independent operator in the 1960s-70s, relied on them either to set casing or to plug and abandon.

> *Looking at that log was just like shooting high dice for $2,500 right then. . . . That was when . . . you [were] fixing to spend some more money. . . . The log was the key, but the anticipation, see, of what that log was going to show was really the thrill of it.*
>
> *We didn't have too many of those [dry holes], because we were either redrilling an old well site or offsetting an old well site where we knew the sand was there, . . . somewhere close. [But] like that sand Tullos is in, it'll cut off right quick. Sometimes in a 100 feet you can't find it. Where it was maybe fifteen feet [from] here, it might be 300 feet from there. Not usually, but that's when we made the dry hole . . . when we didn't get the sand.*
>
> —Max W. Maxwell, 1994

For years, the Hunt companies, Placid Oil, Hunt Petroleum, and H. L. Hunt, along with Cities Service Company, formerly Arkansas Fuel Oil, were the largest producers of Olla oil (SONRIS 2000). But in 1996, PetroHunt bought out Cities Service's holdings, and in 2008, XTO Energy acquired Hunt Petroleum Company's interests. Thus, for half a century, the corporate complexion of Olla's field remained stable, which helped forge historical continuity and family-like solidarity among Olla residents. Hunt and Arkansas Fuel Oil also were the biggies in early Tullos-Urania, but both outfits pulled out over the years, leaving the field to be divided up among a succession of smaller independents. Tullos-Urania has nearly three times as many wells as Olla, but none of today's companies pumping twenty-five or more wells operated there during the early days (SONRIS 2000). Tullos is a ghost of its former self, descendants of its early families long ago departed for greener pastures or the Promised Land.

Olla's oil rush came in without all the rowdiness that fueled Tullos's boom.

> With the country poised on the brink of a war with Japan and Germany, demand for both [lubricating and fuel oil] was sky-high. . . . The strike put Olla's economy, as well as Tullos's, in overdrive. Olla's population more than tripled in just a few years to more than 2,500, its highest ever. James Elliott reported that by the end of 1940, oil payroll accounts deposited in the Olla State Bank had increased by two-thirds in just one year (1995, 23). A single month's payroll late that year totaled nearly a quarter-million dollars.
>
> Business development soared; oil-field service companies broke ground first, followed quickly by stores of all kinds as demand for groceries, goods, and cars turned Olla into a shopping center.
>
> There never was a more timely oil strike than Olla's. The years after the depression left Olla in an austere condition. The Standard mill had closed down. People needed work and money. Oil gave them both. (Gibson 1999, 26)

Olla, the town, was located only eight miles up the road from Tullos, but it might as well have been a hundred. The shock waves from Tullos's boom were greatly attenuated by the time they reached Olla, and when oil was discovered there in 1939, development of the field, though rapid, proceeded in a tranquil fashion, hence the name of Olla's primary producer, Placid Oil Company, formerly H. L. Hunt Oil Company (Elliott 1995, 22-23). Like Urania, Olla had its wild boys and girls who enjoyed Tullos's recreational pursuits, but the adult playgrounds stayed in Tullos.

There is a compelling reason why Olla did not follow Tullos down the path of hooliganism. In 1934, the parish called a vote on a local option for the sale of alcohol, and Olla voted 125 to 83 to stay dry, a decision made easier, no doubt, knowing that Tullos's swinging doors were only ten minutes away (Elliott 1995, 25).

CHAPTER 7

Urania: Life on the Edge of the Commotion

Urania, the town, did not get caught up in the shenanigans rampant just down the road at Tullos. That's because it was a company sawmill town, owned by Henry and Quincy Hardtner (Burns 1999, 37-40). The folks who lived there all worked for the company, and the company took care of them.

Anna Burns relates the Urania experience.

> Employees found all their necessities in the company towns. The owners built a commissary, which served the workers' needs from the "cradle to the grave" with hardware, dry goods, staples, fresh meat, household items, clothes, bolts of cloth, sundries, candy for the children, and even coffins. (Burns 1999, 44)

And they bought on credit.

Everyone lived in a company house and went to company-provided schools, churches, and doctors. Urania had a "Silk Stocking Row" where company "white shirts" had their fancy houses. Flatheads (loggers) and rosinbellies (mill workers) lived in small four-, five-, or rarely six-room, look-alike houses lined-up along outlying gravel roads. Company rules were the law, company bigwigs were judge, jury, and enforcer. Violators were sent packing, after first having their paychecks garnished to settle the commissary bill. Good behavior was expected of children too, but *"if we boys misbehaved enough to get the attention of Quincy Hardtner, he simply called our dad into the office, we got our butts whipped, matter settled."* Urania had no jail, never did, although it did have a town marshal (E. Forrest Cook, pers. comm. 2010). If Urania residents

Mule-drawn log wagon heads for mill after having its load scaled. A single old-growth longleaf pine log fills the wagon and required some mighty stout mules to pull it. The scale house to the right is the large upright hollow log with door. The commissary is in the background. The photograph was taken in 1938 by a Yale University forestry student attending Hardtner reforestation school. The original image is in the Urania Lumber Company Photograph Collection in Durham, North Carolina. (Courtesy of E. Forrest Cook and Town of Urania, Library and Archives, Forest History Society)

frequented Tullos's bars or brothels—and some did—they did so discreetly and at considerable risk to themselves and their families.

Still, Urania lived on the edge of the commotion.

> *Another time, they'd been hijacking them [rig crews and residents living along LA 125] between . . . Tullos and [Olla], right there in that curve like you go to the graveyard there, Pinehill graveyard. . . . Well, me and Gordon Jones — called him Deacon Jones in later years — was coming along there one night, kind of drinking a little bit. Both of us had a gun, and [we] got up there about the Winnfield Road [LA 124] and he [Gordon] said:*
> *"What we gonna do if that guy [the hijacker] walks out?"*
> *"Just pass him a little ways and stop, and I'll get out," Hargrove replied.*
> *Had a nickel-plated thirty-eight. So sure enough, while we was talking, that guy stepped out just past that curve and flagged us.*
> *And I said, "Yes sir, that's him."*
> *So, we went a little ways past, and I jumped out and had that gun, had it*

cocked on him. Couldn't see, it was dark, and I said, "You get in the front."

And he said, "Nawh, I'll ride in the back."

I said, "Nawh, if you're gonna ride, you'll ride in the front. I'm gonna ride in the back."

So, [we] made him get in the front, and we come to Urania. I had that gun on him all time, and it was cocked. And I got to Urania where the lights kind of shined and [he] kinda looked back and got a reflection of that metal. And when we got to Urania [he'd] said he wanted to go to Tullos — that's where we was headed — he said:

"If y'all don't mind, I'll get out here."

I said, "We're going on to Tullos. You can ride to Tullos."

"Nawh, sir."

So we let him out, and that was the last we knew of that, and the last of the holdups.

—Joe Hargrove, 1983

After Tullos's boom began to wane, so did the restrictions, and the few miles separating Urania and Tullos saw a steady stream of pickup trucks trailed by a continual litter of Jax, Falstaff, and Pabst Blue Ribbon bottles.

CHAPTER 8

Out of the Sea

A sense of deep time envelops Tullos. Maybe the oyster shells strewn across the cracked Yazoo clay bring out the feeling, since they are left over from a great salty deluge before land rose out of the sea. Or maybe the feeling comes from images of towering virgin hardwoods darkening the Chickasaw Creek bottom, surreal sights now juxtaposed along a sixty-five-mile-per-hour four-lane and cut-over forests. Urania and Olla mask their age with a mat of pine straw and a botox of traffic lights and open stores. Yet, neatly stacked below pine straw and asphalt lies the story of a titanic struggle between continental and marine forces, a struggle that gave birth to crude oil and humanity's tireless efforts to recover it.

Oil—What Is This Powerful Black Fluid?

What is this powerful black fluid sent from down below? Most geologists are of the opinion that it is the decomposed remains of algae and plankton from ancient oceans, which, over millions of years, were transformed into a decoction of volatile hydrocarbon fluids and gases (Baldwin et al. 2007, 13). On the other hand, some scientists don't believe it is organic at all but comes from subterranean methane gas cooked by the intense heat deep in the belly of the earth (Schlanger 2008, 4). Whatever the origin, oil has charted the destiny of all those who ever sought after it. Tullos, Urania, and Olla have all lived vicariously in the pendulum of its fortunes.

Tullos-Urania oil is brownish-black with a 20 API gravity (Fisk 1938, 188). Gravity expresses the ratio between the weights of equal

Sent from down below. Oil seeps out of a leaking tank on Tullos Heirs lease.
(Photograph by Carla Hallmark)

volumes of freshwater and oil. Water has an API gravity of 10, which equates to a specific gravity of 1.000 and weighs 8.33 pounds per gallon.[1] A gallon of Tullos oil weighs 93.4 percent of a gallon of water, or 7.78 pounds.

> [Tullos oil was] unique because of the low gravity of the oil, very rich. . . . This oil was very heavy and very black, almost green-black. In fact, in the wintertime, to pump out, we had to bypass the valve on the discharge line right near the pump. We had to open this valve when we started to pump oil into the pipeline, gradually closing [the valve] as oil began to move. Sometimes it would be three to four hours before we could close the valve, therefore making pumping time take a lot longer. A 250 barrel tank normally took about three hours to pump out. Bypassing made the time six to seven hours, thereby causing us to have to work longer much of the time. We didn't pay too much mind to time.
>
> —Claude L. Gibson, 1994

Hunt sold it to Harry Sinclair's New York refinery for its cosmetic

Tank battery on Tullos Heirs lease, near Missouri-Pacific railroad, Tullos. (Photograph by Jon Gibson)

properties (H. L. Hunt 1973; quoted by Robert Gray, William Davis, Delbert Noble, pers. comm. 1983) but its ultimate value was as lubricating oil—Pennsylvania-grade motor oil.

Olla oil is black with a 32.5 API gravity (Mike Ganey, pers. comm. 2010), much lighter than Tullos oil. Olla oil weighs 7.19 pounds a gallon, or slightly over a half pound less than a gallon of Tullos oil. Nonetheless, both crudes float on water.

Tullos's Endless River

A matter often discussed over a cup of dark roast at Lessye's Café or debated during domino games at Jack's Pool Hall was where does Tullos's seemingly unending supply of crude oil derive. The field has been producing for more than four score years and shows no signs of going dry.

Well, everybody you ask says they don't know. They got up an idea one

time [that] it's because of the uphill flow of saltwater from the Gulf, floated more stuff in. I heard that, and it [the idea] was pretty prevalent for a long time, but I [suspect] that the oil was just there. . . . It just got broken up so badly with saltwater by so many wells. The structure has been broken up so badly and probably you could find a spot or two in there . . . where you could make a pretty good well, if you knew the field like Frayne [Miles] knew it.
— Max W. Maxwell, 1994

From the Belly of the Earth

The primary oil-producing stratum at Tullos-Urania and Olla is the Wilcox sand (Fisk 1938, 188; Ley et al. 1968, 38-41).[2] It was deposited between 55 million and 65 million years ago (Dockery 1997, 7; Nunn 1986, fig. 1), just after the giant cosmic fireball incinerated the dinosaurs.[3] At Tullos-Urania, oil comes from the upper beds of the Wilcox at depths around 1,500-1,550 feet; at Olla, it comes from the lower beds, around 2,700-2,800 feet deep.

The geological history of Tullos, Urania, and Olla lies moldering in the ground, but it is there for grinding bits and prying eyes to uncover. A duster drilled a few miles south of Tullos hit the top of the Wilcox sand at 1,667 feet and penetrated an additional nineteen feet into the stratum before being plugged (Fisk 1938, 189-90) — notice how sharply the Wilcox dips south of Tullos, better than a hundred feet in just four or five miles (Fisk 1938). Core records from that bore hole show that the Wilcox sediments consisted of alternating beds of lignitic sands and shales, indicating that they accumulated in "a rather broad, flat, swampy coastal plain," periodically drowned by rising sea level (Fisk 1938, 190-91; Ley et al. 1968, 38). Lush tropical vegetation covered the low land. Thick mats of decaying plants collected in shallow still-water lakes and swamps, becoming initially peat and eventually lignite (Haque 2009). Geologist David Dockery (1997, 38) imagines the Wilcox landscape as a shifting jungle-cloaked coastline where sharks, rays, and freshwater gars prowled the estuaries, and crocodiles, terrier-sized antelope-like mammals, and cow-sized marsupial pantodonts roamed the shores.

Layered like a birthday cake atop the Wilcox are sands, greensands, and clays of the Cane River group buried between 1,545 and 1,667 feet deep (Fisk 1938, 190). They were deposited mainly on the seabed. Successively overlying the Cane River sediments are the Sparta, Cook Mountain, and Cockfield strata (Fisk 1938, 188-90; Ley et al. 1968, 41-46). The Sparta sands lie between 1,090 and 1,545 feet deep. They accumulated mainly on land. Above the Sparta, between 801 and 1,090 feet deep, are clays and shales of the Cook Mountain group, which alternatively originated onshore and then offshore. Next comes the predominantly terrestrial Cockfield shales and "rock" between 325 and 801 feet deep (Fisk 1938, 189). The Jackson group comprises the upper 325 feet of sediment (Fisk 1938, 189). Its two superimposed strata—the underlying Moodys Branch marl and the capping Yazoo, or Tullos, clay—formed on the seabed, fairly close to shore, the marl closer to shore than the clay (Beard and Stringer 1995; McPherson and Manning 1986; Schiebout and van den Bold 1986; cf. Fisk 1938, 108).

The saying "old as dirt" applies to these sediments. The Cane River, Sparta, Cook Mountain, and Cockfield beds formed between 41 million and 55 million years ago, and the Jackson group around 34 million and 41 million years ago (Dockery 1997, 7; Nunn 1986, fig. 1). The Moodys Branch marl and Yazoo, or Tullos, clay formed underwater as the Jackson Sea overran the land, raising the ocean depth at Tullos and Urania from 65 feet or shallower to as much as 330 feet (McPherson and Manning 1986, 102; Gary Stringer, pers. comm. 2010). The water grew clearer, the ocean bed finer, and swimmers replaced bottom dwellers as the coastline spread farther and farther north (Beard and Stringer 1995; Nolf and Stringer 2003; Schiebout 1986). Then the region or perhaps the whole world turned increasingly arid, and the Jackson Sea retreated. Tullos went from an open ocean to a lagoon or shallow bay where oysters flourished and first carbonates and then selenite (gypsum) evaporated out of the super-salty sea water.

The Tullos clay was the last major oceanic deposition at Tullos and forms the present-day ground surface. I'm not sure why it isn't buried by later deposits like it is all around—maybe it was and they eroded away or maybe the mighty tectonic hand lifted Tullos higher than they could reach. But, oh, that clay! Sticky enough to ground a marsh buggy but not deep enough to float an airboat, Tullos clay has bogged down all manner of wheeled vehicle from oil field wagon and A-Model to four-wheel-drive pickup and four-wheeler. Old-timers tell of having to wear knee-high boots just to wade across the main street after a rain, and it is claimed that entrepreneurs made a good living charging pedestrians fifty cents to cross the mucky street on their hastily built, temporary boardwalks.

Getting around in Tullos clay sometimes was a matter of talking into a mule's ear.

> *Granddad Evans drove a four-up team . . . pulled pipe where you couldn't get a truck. [One time] Granddad was driving. Uncle Elam Allbritton was with him. And they got bogged down, . . . all four wheels, right down there where our well is [near the Daniels and Goodwin blowout location]. Uncle Elam jumped off the wagon with that whip, and he was going to beat the [mules], and granddad jumped off the wagon too. He said: "If you beat them mules a lick, I'll turn the stock of this buggy whip . . . on you. You don't hit them, you don't work them like that, Elam. Get out of my way, old man, I'll show you how to get a team of ours out." And Uncle Elam said he [granddad] got on the lead mule and . . . reached over and talked in that mule's ear. And he . . . didn't talk but a very few minutes, and he said: "Now, you get us out of here." And he got them out. He [Elam] said, "Boy, that old man learned me something."*
>
> —Clara Belle Evans, 1994

Like scales of a prehistoric reptile, dried-out Tullos clay lines the bottom of a leveed tank overflow pit, Tullos Heirs lease. (Photograph by Carla Hallmark)

Fossil oyster shells, cemented marl-filled burrows, calcium carbonate concretions, and selenite (gypsum) crystals wash out of the scaly Tullos clay and wind up in gullies and saltwater-scalded flats. *Basilosaurus* bones were dug up in a slush pit beside the railroad near the Arkansas Fuel Oil warehouse (Fisk 1938, 89-90; Harris and Veatch 1899, 91-92), and I remember seeing a huge shark tooth, three or four inches long and wide, found in a railroad ditch north of the present-day US Highway 84 overpass. It belonged to a giant *Carcharocles*, easily twice as long as today's great whites.

In the town of Tullos, gullies ran back away from the railroad bed westward toward Castor Creek. Locals called the deepest one, north of the depot, the "Shell Place," because of the seashells and other fossils embedded in the upper two feet of a compact layer exposed in its bed (Fisk 1938, 96, 98-99; Harris and Veatch 1899, 91-92). This layer is greenish-gray, lime-hardened marl, rich in marine fossils (Fisk 1938, 96-98; McPherson and Manning 1986, tab. 2). The marl is an upper layer or lentil in the Tullos (or Yazoo) clay. It is buried by only eight feet of clay, much too close to the top of the ground to be the Moodys Branch formation. Besides, the fossils are typical Tullos, not Moodys Branch, creatures. The layer was

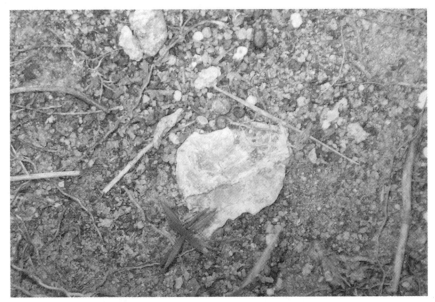

Aged oysters on the half shell at Shelby Loe's bottom field, near Missouri-Pacific railroad and the Shell Place, Tullos. (Photograph by Jon Gibson)

deposited during a fallen sea stand just before waters deepened over Tullos a final time.

Among the treasures from my youth is a Tampa Nugget cigar box full of fossils from that old ditch. Through the good graces of geologist Gary Stringer,[4] these ancient denizens of the deep have been identified giving us a view of what their watery world was like more than 34 million years ago. There are many kinds of gastropods, namely spindle (*Clavilithes humerosus*); tulip (*Latirus* sp.); rock (*Hexaplex marksi*); and moon snails (*Polinices* sp.); horns; sundials (*Architectonica* sp.); turritellids (*Turricula* sp.); volutes (*Athleta symmetricus* and *Lapparia dumosa*); whelks (*Nassarius* sp.); strombids (*Strombus* sp.); the venomous and predatory cone shells (*Conus tortilis*); *Papillinea* sp.; and others, but pelecepods prevail, in particular zigzag clams (*Glycymens pilosa*); scallops (*Chlamys* sp.); *Bathytormus*, and *Pseudoliva vetusta* (Harris 1899, pl. 54, 6-7). Cockles (*Nemocardium nicolletti*) are common too, as are tusk shells (*Dentalium* sp.); shipworms (*Teredo mississippiensis*); and solitary (*Flabellum cuneiforme*) and colonial corals (*Archohelia* sp.) (Fisk 1938, 97-98). Stringer also identified bull (*Carcharhinus gibbesi*); sand (*Odontaspis hopei*); tiger (*Galeocerdo clarkensis*); and mako (*Isurus praecursor*) sharks from their teeth. There are also remains of unspecified bryozoans, crabs, and rays, as well as several caudal vertebrae and ganoid scales of bonyfish.

In a sample taken from a slush pit west of the tracks and north of the depot, probably near the Shell Place, university geologists identified the shells of dozens of different kinds of tiny mollusks, ostracods and forams, and many small clams and snails, as well as teeth and bones of sharks, rays, bonyfish, sea snakes (*Pterosphenus schucherti*), and a petrel-like bird (*Procellariiformes*). Sharks, in addition to those represented at the Shell Place, include nurse (*Ginglymostoma serra*); mackerel (*Lamna* sp.); soupfin or school (*Galeorhinus huberensis*); and lemon (*Negaprion gibbesi*) species. Eagle (*Myliobatis* sp.); duckbilled (*Aetobatis* sp.); and sawshark (*Pristis lathami*) rays are recognized, as are codlet (*Bregmoceras* sp.); barracuda (*Sphyraena major*); cutlassfish (*Trichirus sagittidens*); and billfish (*Cylindracanthus rectus*). And there are two kinds of whales, including the large *Basilosaurus cetoides* and the smaller *Zygorhiza kochii* (Fisk 1938, 97-98; McPherson and Manning 1986, tab. 2).

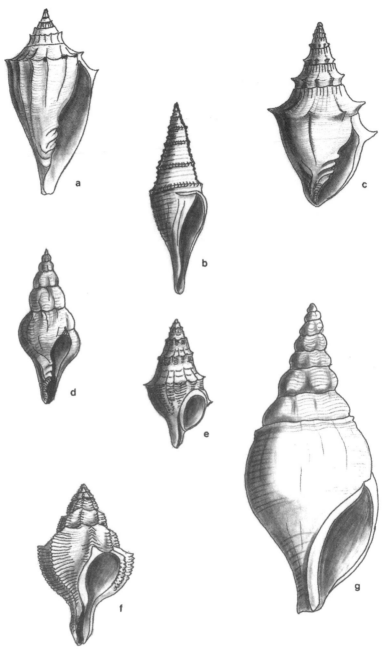

Ancient Eocene gastropods, collected from the Shell Place, near Missouri-Pacific railroad, circa 1950s: a. volute (Athleta symmetricus)*; b. turritellid* (Turricula sp.)*; c. volute* (Lapparia dumosa)*; d. tulip* (Latirus sp.)*; e. Papillinea sp*;*. f. rock* (Hexaplex marksi)*; and g. spindle* (Clavilithes humerosus)*. (Drawing by Jon Gibson)*

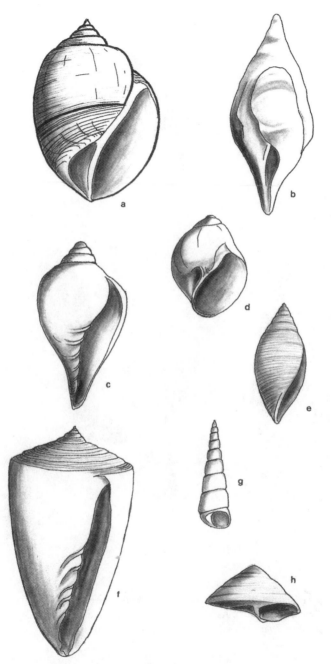

More Eocene gastropods collected from the Shell Place, 1950s: a. moon snail (Polinices sp.); b. unidentified.; c. moon snail (Polinices sp.); d.-e. unidentified; f. cone (Conus tortilis); g. horn; h. sundial (Architectonic sp.). (Drawing by Jon Gibson)

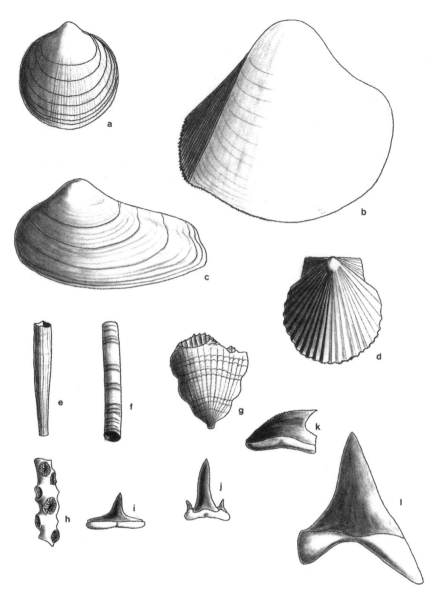

Eocene seashells, coral, and shark teeth, collected from the Shell Place, 1950s: a. cockle; b. zigzag clam; c. Bathytormus; *d. scallop; e. tusk shell* (Dentalium sp.); *f. shipworm; g-h. coral; and i-l. shark teeth.* (Drawing by Jon Gibson)

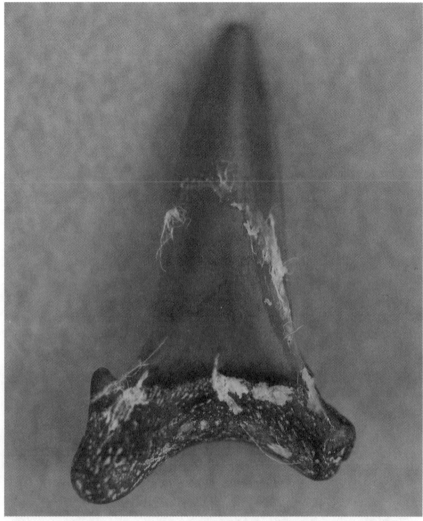

Jaws minus one. Fossil shark tooth from the Shell Place, Tullos. (Photograph by Jon Gibson)

These sea creatures lived close to shore in warm transparent water less than sixty-five feet deep (Gary Stringer, pers. comm. 2010). Corals raised their arms in the filtered blue glow, the seafloor teemed with creeping, crawling, and burrowing bottom dwellers, and colorful fish darted about in the briny, stalked by voracious sharks. And so it was for millions of years, until the sea withdrew from the land for good.

Leviathan

In the summer of 1954, Jimmy Roy Goodwin led a group of us Tullos grade-schoolers to a slush pit west of the railroad track near the Arkansas Fuel Oil warehouse, where his daddy said university geologists had found prehistoric whale bones years before. After pushing our way through the baccharis, we reached the slush pit, fanned out, and began scouring the bare clay looking for bones. I still remember the rush.

It was buried in the khaki-colored clay with only an edge sticking out. I scratched at its sticky clay tomb with a spent welding rod and pried it loose. It rolled halfway down the slush-pit levee before coming to rest. The grayish white object was cylindrical about five inches in diameter and five inches long. The ends were saucer-shaped and the middle was constricted. It was heavy, and where the end was broken, you could see that the inside was porous, like bone. It was bone, a whale backbone, and it had turned into rock.

The vertebra was from a whale all right, originally named *Zeuglodon cetoides* (Fisk 1938, 89-90), now *Basilosaurus cetoides*. *Basilosaurus* was a primitive toothed whale that lived during the Eocene period, 34 million to 41 million years ago. It had a long

Home of the leviathan after eons. Slush pit near location where whale bones were found, Tullos Heirs lease. (Photograph by Jon Gibson)

snout, full of teeth, and a body like an overweight snake, up to seventy feet long, with flippers in front and small vestigial hind legs (Olsen 1959). Like the land-dwelling, four-legged, dog-like creature it descended from, *Basilosaurus* had separate biting and chewing teeth and gulped twenty pounds of sushi—a silver-sided codlet called *Bregmaceros*—each bite. It relished squid for dessert (Carpenter and White 1986).

Remembering the Shell Place

Another fossil-hunting expedition stands out, this one bound for the Shell Place, three-quarters of a mile north of the *Basilosaurus* discovery.

The morning dawned warm and clear. Somewhere down on Tullos Heirs lease, the alternating revving motor of a pulling unit told of a dead well being brought back to life. The freight train bore down, whistle blaring, black smoke billowing. My sisters and

Leviathan: "It's in a book. Daddy showed me." — Jimmy Roy Goodwin, circa 1954, on the finding of fifteen feet of fossil Basilosaurus backbone and some ribs in a Tullos slush pit (Fisk 1938, 90). (Drawing by Jon Gibson)

I walked hurriedly along the shiny rails like tight-rope acrobats. A minute before the locomotive rounded the bend near Placid's loading rack we jumped off the track and clamored down the pile of granite boulders that Southern Pacific had dumped into the deep gully. At the bottom, we stepped onto the narrow shelf of hard gray salt-and-pepper sediment that bordered the shallow saltwater branch, ducked under the suspended barbed-wire fence, and inched our way past the vertical wall of cracked tan clay that buried the gray marl. The shelf widened enough to accommodate us, and we emerged into a magical world we called the Shell Place. Dropping to our knees, pocket knives open, we eyed the embedded seashells, searching for as many different kinds as we could find. We knew the shells and shark teeth were fossils, but what we didn't know then was that we were scratching around in Yazoo (or Tullos) clay, which once was the bed of the warm Jackson Sea some more than 34 million years ago.

Old Natchez Urania & Ruston locomotive No. 3 builds a head of steam, Urania switch yard, early 1940s. (Courtesy of Lane Capps)

Coming 'round the bend. Missouri-Pacific track near the ghost of Hunt's loading rack and the Shell Place. (Photograph by Mike Tradewell)

Underground Structure

Tullos and Urania sit on an underground aneurism, a narrow, two mile-wide, five mile-long, fault-delimited, triskelion-shaped blister on the uppermost Wilcox boundary (Fisk 1938, Pl. XI). The Wilcox formation, or platform, leans steeply toward the southeast, toward the Gulf of Mexico and the Mississippi River canyon, forming a subsurface feature known as a monocline. Tilting began tens of millions of years ago when massive sand deposits began piling up in the Miocene Catahoula delta and gulfward, weighing down the underlying deposits and forcing up those inland (Fisk 1938, 175-77). The blister was raised higher than the general southeast-trending slope and was encircled by a deep, steep-sided, moat-like depression, which enabled oil to gravitate to the higher porous beds at the top of the blister and pool along the many displaced cracks.

Less than five miles southeast of downtown Tullos lies the western flank of the strange Little Creek landform (Echols and McCulloh 2000; Fisk 1938, 177-83), also a producing Wilcox field discovered by Hunt and Justiss (Anonymous 1996a, 5). Little Creek

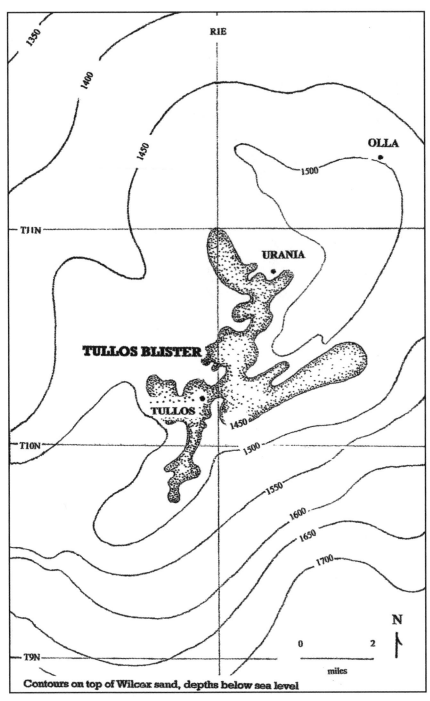

The Tullos subsurface blister. Adapted from Plate XI, Structure Map of the Urania Oil Field (Fisk 1938). (Drawing by Jon Gibson.)

is a dome but, oddly, has a sunken crest. The doughnut-shaped massif is two miles in diameter and is the highest point in LaSalle Parish. Well logs and gravity mapping show the feature rises out of Cretaceous chalk deposits deep underground (Echols and McCulloh 2000, 5). Its origin is a mystery, but several possibilities have been suggested (Echols and McCulloh 2000, 4-6) — a salt dome from which the salt core was pirated causing its inner chamber to crumple, an astrobleme, or ancient deeply buried meteor crater, and a collapsed magma chamber.

Wilcox Oil's Geologic History

We don't know how long ago Tullos-Urania and Olla crudes formed, or how long it took them to form. Their distinctive properties suggest they originated at different times and under different conditions. Olla's oil comes from deeper in the Wilcox formation than Tullos's, which ordinarily would lead us to believe Olla's crude is older. That would be true if the crudes had formed in place, but that's not the way it happened. Oil did not originate in these porous Wilcox beds but seeped into them from elsewhere via a circuitous migration through sand lentils broken up and displaced by crustal warping and faulting. This migration is why Tullos-Urania and Olla fields are still producing long decades after discovery — the endless river of oil has now become a small stream, but it just keeps on rolling along.

CHAPTER 9

Drilling the Tullos-Urania Wilcox

Tullos-Urania oil was shallow, only 1,500 to 1,550 feet deep. The play was in the upper Wilcox formation, an ancient fluvial, deltaic, and offshore deposition that plunged steeply to depths of greater than two miles beneath the waves of the Gulf of Mexico. Giant river canyons, larger than the present-day Mississippi, cut across the ancient Wilcox coastal plain at various places and times delivering their huge flows far out into a then shallower Gulf basin. The old river courses filled in, eventually creating massive bodies of shale in their canyons and separating the Wilcox into distinctive depositional strata (McCulloh and Eversull 1986). One of these old canyons can be traced into central Louisiana, just below the LaSalle Parish line, and might be the reason why oil pooled in the upper Wilcox at Tullos but not at Olla (McCulloh and Eversull 1986, Figs. 1, 4).

Both Tullos-Urania and Olla pools lay within reach of the rotary drilling equipment of the day, but technological advances in detecting oil zones and in preventing well blowouts resulted in Olla's wells being completed in a more controlled, albeit less exciting, fashion.

W. C. McDaniels (pers. comm. 1994) sums up the cutting edge of Tullos's drilling technology when he averred, *"Wasn't no spark plug rigs in them days."*

"Wasn't No Spark Plug Rigs in Them Days"

The earliest drilling rigs in Tullos-Urania were steam-driven.

Yes sir [McDaniels was looking at a photo of the No. 6 discovery well on his living room wall], that's the big steam rig. Wasn't none of them little rigs in them days. [They were] all steam rigs. Wasn't no spark plug rigs in this . . . field in them days.

—W. C. McDaniels, 1994

Initially, wood was used to fire the boilers, but after the first wells were completed, rigs switched to natural, or casinghead, gas. It was fairly simple to convert old wood-fired steam engines to natural gas by replacing the cylinder head and a few minor parts (Caplinger 1997, 33). As old standard rigs began to fall by the wayside in the 1930s and 1940s, gasoline replaced natural gas. Pumping units went to gasoline, too, and eventually to electricity. Olla came in using natural gas or gasoline from the outset.

Old steam drilling and pumping rigs had wooden derricks.

The first derricks were built of heavy lumber by strong, tough, fearless men who held up massive boards with one hand and drove 60-penny spikes with the other. According to Gerald Lynch [1987], . . . old-time rig builders nailed right- and left-handed and drove 60-penny spikes with just three blows from their long-handled nailing hatchets. They were the stuff of legend, their feats exceeded

Tullos fireman and young apprentice prop up against an idle steam boiler. (Courtesy of Ferndale McKeithen and Centennial Cultural Center)

the strength of mortal men. Derrick floor sills usually were 8- by 10-inch timbers, and floors were rough 3- by 12-inch boards. Derrick legs usually were made from 2- by 8-inch finished boards nailed together with 30-penny nails. Legs were joined by 2- by 12-inch girts, and 2- by 6-inch sway braces were nailed to derrick legs between girts. Girts controlled taper, and derricks on Tullos-Urania leases normally were 84 or 96 feet tall, tall enough for stands of pipe to be stacked upright inside derricks (Gibson 1999, 49; also see Lynch 1987, 6, 10).

At Tullos, steel derricks began to replace wooden ones during the 1930s and 1940s, but from the outset, Olla's derricks were made of steel.

"Back in them days, they was all wooden derricks, you know. They [drilling outfit] had a derrick man [rig builder], and they put up the derricks ahead [of time]. The derrick was already there when you moved in." — W. C. McDaniels, 1994. (Photograph by S. G. Wilson, courtesy of Lorraine Byrd and Luther Byrd)

Steel derrick and powerhouse, unknown location, Tullos-Urania field, early 1930s. The original image is in the Urania Lumber Company Photograph Collection in Durham, North Carolina. (Courtesy of E. Forrest Cook and Town of Urania, Library and Archives, Forest History Society).

Steel derrick of abandoned well rises above Chickasaw bottom along LA Highway 125 near Urania. (Photograph by Jerry Harris)

Steel derrick blanketed with rare snow, LA 125, near Chickasaw Creek. (Photograph by Carla Hallmark)

Saplings and liana swallow steel derrick on E. W. Nugent Place, Olla. (Photograph by Jon Gibson)

As the Rotary Turns

Once the derrick was erected, it only took eight to ten days to drill to the top of the Wilcox (W. C. McDaniels, pers. comm. 1994). Before the rotary ever turned, the location was prepared and drilling equipment hooked up. Equipment was hauled in by wagon, later by truck (Sonny King, pers. comm. 2010; also see Lynch 1989, 11-15).

Roughnecks dug a slush pit nearby to hold drilling mud. If no creek was handy, they also dug a pit to hold water for the boiler. They hookedup the drawworks on one side of the rig floor and, on the other side of the rig, some distance away, connected the steam engine and boiler. Drawworks bore the hoisting gear. A big spool, or bullwheel, held the drilling line, or cable, which was strung up and over a fixed set of pulleys on top of the derrick, or crown block, and then back down to the traveling block—a heavy set of sheaves pulled up and down by the drilling line as the driller engaged the brake on the drawworks.

When preparing to drill, the crew hung a big hook from the traveling block and suspended a swivel beneath the hook with a bail. The swivel housed a rotating sleeve, which allowed the suspended drill string to spin without twisting and tangling the block and line. A mud hose was run into the top of the sleeve in the swivel and was bolted in place, and the Kelly joint, the topmost joint of pipe on the drill string, was bolted to the bottom of the swivel. Unlike regular tubular drill pipe, the Kelly joint was square or hexagonal and was twenty-eight, thirty-eight, or, sometimes, sixty feet long. It fit into a square hole lined with bushings in the rotary table, a heavy, flat, circular appliance mounted in the center of the well floor. A chain drive from the engine turned the rotary, which, in turn, spun the Kelly and the connected drill string.

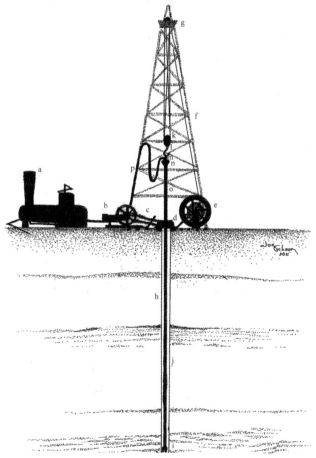

Steam drilling rig assembly: a. boiler; b. engine; c. drive chain; d. rotary table; e. bullwheel; f. derrick; g. crown block; h. drill string; i. fishtail bit; j. annulus; k. traveling block; l. swivel; m. big hook; n. elevator; o. Kelly joint; and p. stand pipe. (Drawing by Jon Gibson)

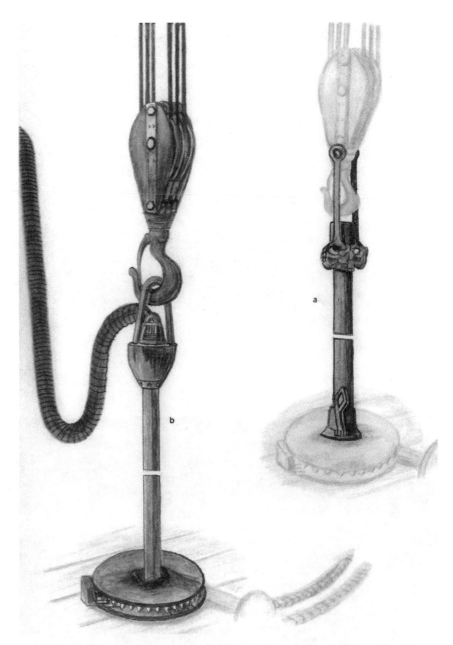

Hooked up for drilling. a. making up, or adding, joints to drill string; b. making hole, or drilling. (Drawing by Jon Gibson)

Their last trip made, traveling block, big hook, and swivel find final rest at M lease, Tullos. (Photograph by Jon Gibson)

Swivel retired from swiveling, King Drilling Company yard, Tullos. (Photograph by Carla Hallmark)

Discarded rotary table, King Drilling Company yard, Tullos. (Photograph by Carla Hallmark)

The driller drove the rig by working the clutch and brake. The drill string was heavy, especially in later years, after drill collars were added above the bit. By applying or easing off on the brake, the driller reduced or increased torque on the spinning drill string, thereby controlling the rate of drilling. As drilling progressed, new joints of drill pipe had to be continually added to the drill string. Each time a joint was added, the Kelly with attached swivel was withdrawn from the borehole, uncoupled, and stuck in the nearby rat hole to get it out of the way. An elevator—a heavy-duty, hinged, pipe-gripping clamp—was hung on the outside ears of the traveling block by means of a sturdy set of eyed pins. From his lofty perch on the monkey board up in the derrick, the derrickman then guided the elevator to the pipe stand where he latched onto a joint of drill pipe. The gripped joint was then raised, swung over the rotary table, and stabbed into the collar of the last downhole joint of drill pipe, which was held fast by slips mounted in the rotary table. After making up the joints, the string was lowered into the borehole until the slips caught the collar on the top joint. The elevator was unlatched and pushed aside, slips removed, and traveling block sent back to the derrickman who reattached the swivel and Kelly. The Kelly was then maneuvered into the drive bushings in the rotary table, and drilling proceeded another pipe-length deeper until pay sand was reached.

Oil field soap opera. Justiss-Mears driller, Jim Woodruff, watches as the rotary turns, early 1940s. (Courtesy of Jennifer Loe, Justiss Oil Company)

A rat hole is not for rats but Kelly joints. Olla discovery well, Louisiana Central Oil and Gas No. 9. (Photograph by Jon Gibson)

Hung from the traveling block, elevators clamped onto collared pipe enabling it to be raised or lowered in the drill hole (Lynch 1987, 14). King Drilling Company yard, Tullos. (Photograph by Carla Hallmark)

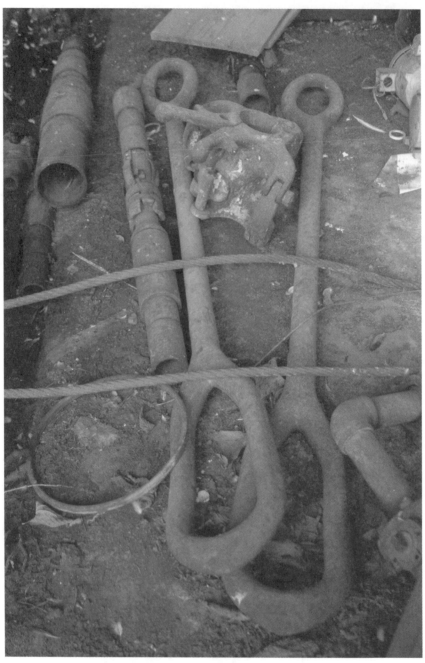

Eyed pins once connected elevator to traveling block while tripping. King Drilling Company yard, Tullos. (Photograph by Carla Hallmark)

Slips fit into the bushing on the rotary table. They gripped and held pipe stationary when "breaking out" or "making up" joints. As old-time oil man Gerald Lynch (1987, 15) remarked "If the 'slips' slip, they are not doing their job." King Drilling Company yard, Tullos. (Photograph by Carla Hallmark)

Joints of tubing lie on pipe rack. Sonny King Drilling Company yard, Tullos. (Photograph by Carla Hallmark)

Drilling mud was pumped from the mud pit into the stand pipe mounted on the well floor. From the stand pipe, it flowed through the flexible mud hose and into the swivel. From the swivel, it ran down the Kelly joint and drill pipe to the fishtail bit, where it gushed out through nozzles mounted on both sides of the bit's blades. Mud flushed drill cuttings up the annulus—the space between the pipe and the sides of the borehole—and out through a return mud line onto a shaker screen where loose cuttings were caught. The screened mud flowed back into the mud pit and was reused.

After the well reached bottom, or total depth (TD), drill pipe was removed and casing was run down the bore hole. Cement was pumped down the casing. It oozed out of the bottom of the casing and spread back up the annulus. This stopped cave-ins and also kept out unwanted water. After the cement set, it was drilled out of the casing. In early wells, the lowest joint of casing was fitted with a screen on the bottom, or else a slotted or perforated joint of pipe was set in the production sand.[1] Then, smaller diameter pipe, or tubing, was run inside the casing from the well floor to the production zone, and a string of sucker rods was run inside the tubing. Rods connected the walking beam on the surface pump to the working barrel, or downhole pump, which bore the cups that picked up the fluid that seeped into the tubing.

Joints of casing hide beneath carpet of smartweed, goldenrod, and Chinese tallow. King Drilling Company yard, Tullos. (Photograph by Carla Hallmark)

Mobile Drilling and Workover Rigs

If the well was brought in, drilling derricks were left in place and pumping equipment installed. If the well was dry or sanded up, wooden derricks would often be moved, or skidded, to a nearby location, an enormous feat for man and mule/winch truck. The derrick had to be jacked up, heavy planking laid down, roller logs placed on the planks, and mule teams or trucks started towing the derrick toward the new location. Once skidding started, it was an anathema to stop as kinetics made it nearly impossible to get the rig moving again. The board road was laid at a frenzied pace—men picking up the already-crossed planks and logs and rushing to lay them in front of the slowly moving derrick until reaching the new drilling site. Mules made the best mudders, as winch trucks, even though low-geared, simply bogged down.

Many derricks were left standing long after the wells played out and furnished a handy source of lumber, pipe, and parts, but that began to change in the 1950s and 1960s. Mobile drilling and workover rigs began to remake the skyline of the oil field. Standing derricks and powerhouses disappeared. Outfits literally drove their trailered drilling or truck-mounted workover rigs to a location, raised their masts or gin poles, drilled or repaired a well, and then drove the rig to a new location. Hooking up portable pumping units at the wellhead gave a low, roomy look to what had always seemed a tall, crowded, derrick-filled land.

Drilling Mud

In the early days at Tullos, drilling mud was really just plain old mud, made by roughnecks wading barefooted in a water-filled pit (Williams 1976, 6). But heavier mud was needed to suppress the higher pressure in Olla's deeper wells, and clever well-makers found the solution in a clay mineral called Bentonite (Langenkamp 2006, 30), which was able to absorb up to eight times its own weight in water. This heavy, water-logged mud was pumped down the wells as needed to control high gas pressure in the borehole and cool off fast-spinning, sizzling hot drill bits.[2]

Taking a break. Disconnected engine alongside workover unit with telescoping mast pulling rods in Tullos, LA Highway 125. (Photograph by Jon Gibson)

Telescoping mast of a 1967 Spencer Harris 3500 trailered drilling rig reaches for the sky. Powered by Caterpillar diesels and pulled by an International Harvester truck, this rig was run by Sonny King, who drilled more than 500 wells with it, the last in 1977. Sonny King Drilling Company yard, Tullos. (Photograph by Carla Hallmark)

"*Red Dawg*" *workover unit preparing to repair parted rods in the MWM Energy Company Kyle-Davis No. 1 well (Serial No. 9400), located near the First Baptist Church in old downtown Tullos. The first status report on the well was filed on November 24, 1975, and a drilling permit issued later, July 1, 1976 (SONRIS 2000), which suggests that drillers cleaned out an old dead well. This conclusion is supported by the lack of a spud date and production depth in SONRIS records, coupled with the use of a serial number, which should have been assigned to wells drilled in early 1926. On-site archaeological investigations by Robert Ivy and me in July 2011 found remnants of burned-down walls of a belt hall confirming that an old standard rig once stood at the location.* (Photograph by Jon Gibson)

Coring

In the early days, coring — or taking solid "rock" samples, or cores, from the wellbore — was done to let drillers know when they were getting close to pay sand, but interpreting those samples inspired little confidence, mainly because, according to Joe Hargrove: "*They [geologists] didn't know what they were talking about.*" Hargrove relates how he once handed a city-slicker geologist a lump of hard mud (others claim it was dried-up dog dung), and the geologist bit it in two, proclaimed it to be chalk, and excitedly announced that oil was near. The well was dry.

W. C. McDaniels shared a similar lack of faith.

> *Well, they had a rig [core barrel] there they'd run down there [drill hole] and take a core. They knew about where it [the sand] was. They'd stop maybe fifty feet above there and go to coring. Back there then the core barrel was eight feet long, . . . and you run it down there . . . take a core and look at*

it. That's all they had. Awh, they had mud-eaters — [that's] what they called
them back in them days — [they'd] set there and catch samples coming out,
you know. . . . Every rig had one of them.
— W. C. McDaniels 1994

Later, coring carried out along with remote logging became a
reliable means of identifying potential oil-bearing strata, especially
after sidewall coring came into use (Mike Ganey, pers. comm. 2010).
Instead of taking a long continuous core, sidewall coring fires a
hollow "bullet" through the tubing into the formation. The plugged
"bullet" is tethered to a wireline, reeled to the surface, and inspected.

Drill Bits

Drill bits are the hardened steel cutting head on the bottom of
the drill string. The first bits used at Tullos were called fishtail bits
because their side-by-side cutting blades resembled a fishtail. They
bore small nozzles between the blades where drilling mud was jetted
from a surface pump forcing loose scrapings back up the annulus
and cooling off the bit. They were replaced in the 1930s by roller-cone
bits. These ingenious cutting heads had two or three independently
rotating cones armed with teeth that intermeshed as the cones
turned. Designed for cutting through rock and hard sediments, they
made short work of Tullos's and Olla's sands and clays.

Two-bladed fishtail bit. Note mud nozzle and welded drill collar, King Drilling
Company yard, Tullos. (Photograph by Carla Hallmark)

Three-bladed fishtail bit, King Drilling Company yard, Tullos. (Photograph by Carla Hallmark)

Roller tri-cone bit rusts away on abandoned popup drilling rig on Tullos Heirs lease. (Photograph by Carla Hallmark)

When early drill bits broke or became dull or twisted, they were sent to a bit shop, or smithy, for refurbishing. Not only was the work hot and hard, it was dangerous — blowing open fires, flying sparks, and sizzling red-hot iron in a volatile environment of oil puddles and natural gas pockets. In addition, shops were often stuck in the midst of closely spaced wells in order to speed repair turn-around time, making them vulnerable to boiler mishaps at nearby rigs.

> *I went to strapping at this bit shop. Well, it's where they hammered out these bits, fishtail bits, and fishing tools, and so forth like that. . . . Well, I worked that day, and blood blisters come in my hands, and blood came through my gloves. . . . Next morning, I picked up that sledge hammer, and tears come in my eyes. . . . He [fellow strapper, Cotton Weems] was taking them [bits] out of the fire and flipping them. This old big one [Mac, the three-hundred-pound shop owner] saw me and said: "Well, son, let me tell you something. If that don't kill you, it'll make a man out of you."*
> —Joe Hargrove, 1983

> *We had a bit shop down there in town, and they'd [drillers] get one of them bits they used on a rock or something or other [some obstruction in the bore hole] and knock it off. [They] changed bits, you know. Put it [the broken bit] in the shop. . . . Get it hot and whip it back out to the right size. . . . If you're going to set seven-inch casing, you got to have it big enough for that [bit] to go down. . . . Awh, it's changed a lot since then though.*
> —W. C. McDaniels, 1994

One deadly explosion flattened McManan's Machine Works in Tullos. The enormous blast killed one worker, splintered lumber, twisted pipe, crumpled boiler plate, knocked down trees, and severely damaged a nearby well. Although the circumstances of this disaster are long forgotten, it is generally believed that a ruptured boiler was to blame.

Many old steam boilers were lost, not through fireman carelessness but because saltwater managed to get into the boiler — an omnipresent danger because, by this time, all nearby water sources, creeks and pits, were pure brine. When heated, saltwater foamed so badly that firemen couldn't tell exactly how much water was in the boiler (Lynch 1987, 63). If the water level dropped below the crown sheet, the sheet would get red hot and, then, when cold water was added to the boiler and touched the sizzling plate, the result was explosive, often tragic.

Firing boilers earned big bucks but was not a highly sought-after job. Gerald Lynch (1987, 64) tells of turning on the boiler's water

Explosion destroys Tullos bit shop, the same bit shop remembered by Joe Hargrove and W. C. McDaniels. (Courtesy of Lorraine Byrd and Luther Byrd)

Twin boilers hooked up and letting off steam. (Courtesy of Jennifer Loe, Justiss Oil Company)

injector and then running like mad to hide behind a nearby tree in case the water level was too low. It made him so nervous he quit firing boilers before completing his second well.

"Awh, it's changed a lot since then though"

In just over a decade, drilling went from using wood-fired steam power and fishtail bits to using natural gas and gasoline power and rotary bits. Wooden derricks gave way to steel derricks and eventually to mobile rigs with popup masts. Drilling mud changed from mudhole mud to Bentonite mud and cores from the "mud-eater" variety to the wireline plugged-bullet type. But oil came from the same pay sand — the upper Wilcox formation 1,500 to 1,550 feet down — and, now, eight decades after discovery, oil men are still profiting from it. Tullos's boom has finally quieted, but those wild days of yore are remembered whenever old hardhats gather for morning coffee.

CHAPTER 10

Keep on Pumping

After drilling was completed, casing set, and rod string connected, Tullos-Urania wells were ready for the pump—gas pressure in the upper Wilcox simply was too low to sustain free-flow for long, even when wells blew out.

The Pumping Assembly—Steam Rigs

Roustabouts rigged up the pumping assembly. They connected a boiler to a single cylinder steam engine and built a wooden, or tin, shed over the engine. With the boiler cooking, the engine drove a big, wide vulcanized-fabric belt wound around a vertical wooden bandwheel. The belt and wheel assembly was housed inside a belt hall, an elongated building, which ran from the engine shed to the derrick, often called the powerhouse. The metal shaft in the center of the spinning bandwheel turned a crank, which ran outside the belt hall through a narrow opening in the wall where it connected with the Pittman arm on the surface pump at the wellhead.

The Pittman was attached to the hard-nose end of a wooden walking beam centered on a Sampson post and brace. A bridle attached to the other end of the walking beam was connected to the polished rod, the slick uppermost end of the long string of sucker rods, which ran inside the tubing from the stuffing box to the bottom of the well (Sonny King, pers. comm. 2010).

As the crank turned round and round, it pushed-pulled the walking beam up and down, alternately lifting and lowering the polished rod and attached rod string. This allowed oil to seep into the downhole pumping, or working, barrel on the upstroke. On the downstroke, the rod string plunged into the barrel, filling its cups with oil. The ensuing upstroke lifted the precious fluid toward the surface. As oil reached the top of the tubing, it was bled off by a take-off line and run into an open storage pit or lease tank. Casinghead gas was carried off by another line and was usually flared, unless used to fire the boiler or run stoves and space heaters in nearby residences, and just about everybody in the town of Tullos and in the Olla oil field cooked and heated with casinghead gas—it was free.

Steam rig pumping assembly: a. engine; b. engine shed; c. bandwheel belt; d. bandwheel; e. Pittman arm; f. Sampson post; g. walking beam; h. powerhouse; i. headache post; j. stuffing box; k. polish rod; l. bullwheel; m. derrick; n. crown block; o. cellar; p. drill hole with casing; and q. working barrel. (Drawing by Jon Gibson)

One of two wooden bandwheels still standing in Tullos. Located along the north side of US Highway 84 just west of the intersection with US Highway 165. (Photograph by Carla Hallmark)

Old standard pumping rig rises above barren Tullos terrain, circa late 1920s. Belt hall hides bandwheel and big belt. Supported by Sampson post, Pittman arm raised and lowered walking beam. The original image is in the Urania Lumber Company Photograph Collection in Durham, North Carolina. (Courtesy of E. Forrest Cook and Town of Urania, Library and Archives, Forestry History Society)

Metal shaft and crank on bandwheel, manufactured by Parkersburg Rig and Reel Company, Parkersburg West Virginia. (Photograph by Carla Hallmark)

Polish rod slides through stuffing box pulling crude from the formation to the surface, MWM Energy Company Miles Heirs Lease No. 1. US Highway 84 at Missouri-Pacific railroad, Tullos. (Photograph by Jon Gibson)

Steam-driven standard rigs pump crude into open storage pits, Tullos-Urania field, circa late 1920s. The original image is in the Urania Lumber Company Photograph Collection in Durham, North Carolina. (Courtesy of E. Forrest Cook and Town of Urania, Library and Archives, Forestry History Society)

New growth claims rusty lease tank on F. M. Keys Lease, Olla. (Photograph by Jon Gibson)

Lease Tanks Peep through Window of Pyracantha, Loblolly Pine, and Baccahris on Tullos Heirs Lease, Tullos. (Photograph by Jon Gibson)

Walking Beams

A walking beam is the wooden or metal arm on the oil well pump assembly, which moves up and down and brings crude oil to the surface (Langenkamp 2006, 488). The hard-nose end of the walking beam is connected to a Pittman arm, which is pulled back and forth by an engine-driven crank, often counter-weighted in later times. The other end (sometimes bearing a horsehead) is connected by a bridle, or loop of cable, to a rod string that runs inside the tubing all the way down to the oil-bearing formation. A fulcrum called a Sampson post supports the beam. As the crank turns, the Pittman raises and lowers the walking beam like a see-saw. The motion alternatively pulls and pushes the rod string through the tubing and pumps oil from the formation.

In Tullos, Tom Russell turned out wooden walking beams and lumber for wooden derricks, belt halls, and the like.

> *"There's a lot of Russells here [in Tullos], you know, but this one [Tom Russell] he made a lot of walking beams and stuff like that," recalled W. C. McDaniels.*
>
> *"He . . . kept them on the yard, and when they needed some, they'd go down there to Tom's place," added Jesse E. Albritton.*
>
> *"Go get them a walking beam or timbers, you know. . . . Those standard*

Retired walking beam, Pittman arm sunning, and Sampson post still hefting, King Drilling Company yard, Tullos. (Photograph by Carla Hallmark)

Abandoned Lufkin walking beam bearing horsehead rises above swaying goldenrods, King Drilling Company yard, Tullos. (Photograph by Carla Hallmark)

rigs, they had timber in there. Didn't [use] no concrete . . . just put timbers. They made big wedges, to wedge them things [derricks] in there. They was all standard rigs in them days," continued McDaniels.

"When they built this church [Tullos First Baptist, the new brick building downtown], Tom give $10,000 and some property. And they built that church they got here," said Albritton.

"And old Doodle White [Hollis Mixon White] worked for him. They might have been kin, I don't know, but he [Doodle] went to selling beer. He was the first one that went to selling beer in Tullos, old Doodle White," remarked McDaniels.

— W. C. McDaniels and Jesse E. Albritton, 1994

Air Lifting

Besides standard belt-hall pumping rigs and portable pumping units, Tullos-Urania tried several other means of pumping oil out of the ground. Air lifting was one, and an outfit named Air Lift operated about a half mile north of the discovery well location on Chickasaw Creek, just east of the old road (LA 125) in the south limits of Urania. Compressed air was jettisoned into wells by "wind jammers" forcing fluid up the tubing, where it was then blown into open pits (Wall 1983, 5A). Pumps skimmed off the crude and sent it to "treaters," where oil, water, and basic sediments were separated and the clean oil (less than two percent BS&W) stored in tanks awaiting shipment by rail to Lake Charles refineries (Claude Gibson, pers. comm. 1994). Air lifting was discontinued when it was realized that the pressurized air pushed as much oil away from the production zone as into it (Anonymous 1945, 5).

Central Powers and Shackle Lines

Central powers were also used in Tullos-Urania, but not in Olla (Clark 1983, 10B; Wall 1983, 5A). There were three powers—one on the Tullos Heirs lease, a second on the S. Tullos lease behind the Princess movie theater, and a third on the M lease near the Arkansas Fuel Oil picnic grounds on the northern outskirts of Tullos.

Tullos's central powers pumped as many as eight or ten wells at once by connecting distant pumping units to a big, centrally located, flat-lying bullwheel, mounted on an eccentric (Gibson 1999, 52; Wall 1983, 5A). When the big Superior engine turned the wheel, it imparted a reciprocating push-pull motion to the connecting lines, or shackle lines (called "shak-a-lines" in the local vernacular). Shackle lines were lengths of wire rope or screwed-together sucker rods suspended two to three feet off the ground by short wooden friction posts. The back and forth motion of the lines pulled down the Pittman arm of the pumps and drove the wells.

Shackle lines screeched noisily as they rubbed across the periodically oiled friction posts providing constant background noise in town. When the screeching stopped, everyone knew the power was down and needed repair. Tullos native and former Justiss-Mears roughneck, Tom Henslee, remembers shackle lines being used to hone youngsters' balance: *"We used to stand on the rods as they moved on the ground, about two feet one way, then back."*

Gasoline Pumping Units

As time wore on, gasoline pumping units replaced the old standard steam rigs. Initially mounted under derricks, the advent of mobile workover units and their gin poles rendered derricks obsolete, and Tullos and Olla became a land of bobbing steel pumpers in continual motion.

Abandoned pumper on Urania B lease, Urania. (Photograph by Jon Gibson)

Head held high, Tullos Heirs pumping unit puts Wilcox crude in the line, Tullos. (Photograph by Jon Gibson)

Ruins of old standard rig. Hardtner No. 2 (Serial No. 9121). Spudded December 23, 1925, and plugged December 1, 1976, after fifty-one years of production. (Photograph by Jon Gibson)

Today, electricity quietly drives Tullos-Urania's old rust-encrusted, oil-stained pumpers. It also powers Olla's pumping units, even though they usually sport a fresh coat of paint.

Pulling Rods

Sometimes, sucker or pumping rods come apart down in the hole, and roustabouts must repair the break, a job usually referred to as "pulling rods." Joby McBroom, a tool pusher for Glen D. Loe Oil Company, explains to a green hand, or "boll weevil," how to go about "tailing rods," which entails pulling the rods out of the tubing and unscrewing and stacking them beside the derrick or workover unit (Langenkamp 2006, 439).

Joby McBroom (pers. comm. 1965) gives an on-the-job tutorial on how to tail rods.

> *All you have to do is grab onto the end of the rod, and when I let the breadbasket [traveling block] down, you run hard as you can out there and lay the rod on the ground and the boys will uncouple. Then you run back up there and grab ahold of the next rod and tail it out there so that it lays down right next to the first rod. And then you go get another and another and keep on like that until we get down to where the rods are parted. Usually we pull doubles, but today we're pulling tribbles so we can beat the rain. That means instead of uncoupling every second rod, we'll be uncoupling every third one. Ain't going to be no problem for a young war-horse like you, is it kid?*
>
> – Joby McBroom

Going Fishing

Fishing tools are contraptions lowered down a well on the end of the rod or tubing string in order to "grab" onto any obstructing object and bring it out of the hole; e.g., a joint of pipe that "backed off" (became unscrewed) downhole, an eaten-up working barrel, a worn-out packer or tubing anchor, or even a pipe wrench accidently kicked in the hole (Robert Lurry, pers. comm. 2010). "Worming" stunts were commonplace on well floors, and fishing tools often saved the day, as well as worms' (klutzs') jobs.

Racked sucker rods. King Drilling Company yard, Tullos. (Photograph by Carla Hallmark)

Changing Cups

Cups are concave discs made of vulcanized fabric that fit around the traveling valve in downhole sucker-rod pumps, or working barrels). When the sucker-rod string is being pulled upward by the surface pump, oil seeps into the downhole pump barrel, or standing valve, at the bottom of the well. On the ensuing down stroke, a plunger, or traveling valve, pushes into the pump barrel filling the cups and, on the upstroke, lifts the oil up the tubing to the surface.

> *We had three crews [workover gangs — roustabouts] that kept the rods pulled, which meant you changed the cups. . . . The cups on the rod pick up the fluid. If you keep the water out of the production pipe, then that keeps the pressure off of the oil sand. The water pressure, the water weight . . . will keep the oil sand from coming in 'cause it's lighter. If you keep that pulled off, then that oil can come in. So we changed those cups as frequently as we could, sometimes more than once a month. And we got our production up to four barrels.[1]*

> —Max W. Maxwell, 1994

Discarded cup removed from working barrel of MWM Energy's Kyle-Davis No. 1 well, old downtown Tullos. (Photograph by Jon Gibson)

Gravel Packing

One other thing [that kept production up]: We did what we called gravel packing. . . . They washed out . . . a big hole in the sand in the bottom of the well below the pipe where they were producing from . . . and then they packed it full of gravel. Well, that gravel kept the water from coming in so badly, and the oil could seep in a little easier. In fact, we took some wells that were down to only making a barrel or two a day . . . pushed them up to making eleven barrels a day down on Castor Creek, just by gravel packing. And they kept up that production for six, seven, or eight months, and then they'd [wells] start easing off again because the gravel would be moved because of the movement of the fluid through the gravel.

— Max W. Maxwell, 1994

Deafening by Its Absence

Today, electricity quietly drives Tullos-Urania and Olla pumping units. One Tullos outfit, S. H. Loe Oil Corp., even generates its own electricity. Except when occasionally interrupted by the sound of a revving pulling unit somewhere, the old familiar heavy-metal cacophony led by the pumping units is deafening by its absence. Nonetheless, just as fast as pumping units withdraw the oil, nature replenishes it.

CHAPTER 11

Running Oil: From Field to Refinery

In Tullos-Urania, green, or untreated, oil[1] was pumped from lease tanks or open pits to a treating plant where basic sediments and water (BS&W) were removed (Anonymous 1945, 5; Claude L. Gibson, pers. comm. 1994). It was then pumped into large storage tanks awaiting shipment. There were no pipelines to carry Tullos-Urania and Olla crude directly to refineries in Lake Charles, so Tullos-Urania oil was loaded on tank cars and transported by rail. Olla's was trucked to Jonesville where it was loaded on barges and taken by pusher boat down the Black River to the Red and then down the Mississippi to refineries in Baton Rouge (Claude L. Gibson, pers. comm. 1994; W. C. McDaniels, pers. comm. 1994).

Abandoned large storage tank once witnessed busy days at nearby Hunt's loading rack, now MWM Energy Miles Heirs Lease, Tullos. (Photograph by Jon Gibson)

Lease tanks gather crude on Tullos Heirs lease, near the old Ben Long place, Tullos. (Photograph by Jon Gibson)

Their fires long extinguished, oil treaters nap on a carpet of ragweed and smartweed in King Drilling Company yard, Tullos. (Photograph by Carla Hallmark)

Arkansas Pipeline Co. employee Claude L. Gibson ran Tullos-Urania oil during the late 1940s and 1950s, and he describes the way the process worked.

> We [Arkansas Pipeline Corporation] bought this . . . green oil—the only place I know of that oil was handled like this. Shorty Taylor worked for Arkansas Fuel Oil and treated oil through two boilers, the first temperature about 180 degrees and the other about 220 degrees. This along with chemicals separated the BS&W from the oil. . . . After treating one day, the water and sediment went to the bottom of the tank, which we bled off the next morning. There was a suction line on the tank about one to two inches from the bottom which had a valve to open and close when the oil was ready.
> —Claude L. Gibson, 1994

From the large storage tanks, oil was piped to loading racks. Gibson started the big wheels turning.

> Pipeline oil below 2 percent BS&W was loaded. We turned the tank on, then went to the pump station room and started the engine, which was a twenty-five horsepower Superior engine with two big wheels head high. To start the engine, we had to open the mixing chamber, put gasoline in, and set the Waco to fire just off center. Then we rode the big wheel down until it fired and started. Before this, however, we put a dog nut on the oval connection on the rear of the engine to make . . . the engine easier to roll over. After the engine started, we removed the dog nut. We gradually turned on the natural gas. . . . Then we opened the discharge valve outside and came back in and moved the clutch in to start the pump, which had a large belt about ten-inches wide on a pulley from the engine to the pump. This belt was run straight on the engine and pump, which enabled the pump to pump in a forward motion. You could cross the belt in a figure eight and the pump would run in a backward motion. Funny, isn't it?
> —Claude L. Gibson, 1994

The engine started the oil flowing toward the loading rack. The loading rack was a raised walkway alongside a railroad siding where oil run from large storage tanks was transferred into waiting tank cars. Gibson continues:

> Meanwhile, . . . someone had taken a man to the loading rack to open . . . at least two tank cars. The oil came in under the rack in

"Twenty-five horsepower Superior engine with two big wheels head high." — Claude Gibson. Located at King Drilling Company warehouse, Tullos. (Photograph by Carla Hallmark)

an eight-inch line. There were three-inch lines [with] connections on top of the line about every ten feet apart. These riser lines came up under the rack to [a height of] about eight feet, on top of the rack. There was a valve about four feet from the top of the rack so oil flow could be opened or closed off. A four-inch piece of blow pipe . . . was slipped over the iron pipe, which had a swivel at the top so it could be swung around, up or down, to maneuver [into] the dome opening of the railroad car. The blow pipe had . . . a 45-degree elbow so it would allow oil to go into the car. Then when the valve was turned . . . loading began. We had to take temperature and get BS&W checks at intervals. Tank cars held about 240 barrels, or about 10,080 gallons. The pump at the pump station pumped about 240 an hour. It took about one hour to load each car.

—Claude L. Gibson, 1994

Once the oil started moving toward the loading rack, there was no off stitch.

Oil was pumped through a six-inch line approximately four miles from the [pumping] station to the loading rack [Denkman's]. About 9:30 or 10:00 a.m., I would go down to Dean's Grocery Store and drink a coke

Arkansas Pipeline Company man, Claude Gibson, prepares to run oil into waiting tank car at Denkman loading rack, in Rochelle circa early 1950s. (Photograph by Kathren Maxwell Gibson)

(price, five cents). After I had fixed the oil to go into two empty cars, I would have plenty of time without hurrying. You could not ever turn off the flow of oil—had to keep the valves open so as not to blow the line apart. We would load seven or eight cars a day, so we had time in the eight hour period. We had no lunch hour, just kept loading all the time.

—Claude L. Gibson, 1994

Four loading racks serviced the Tullos-Urania field: Denkman's in Rochelle, Hunt's and Arkansas Fuel Oil's in Tullos, and Urania's.

For years and years, Tremont and Gulf Railroad from Winnfield pulled the empty cars alongside the rack, then pulled the filled cars up to Denkman Station at Rochelle to be routed to the Lake Charles refinery via the Missouri & Pacific Railroad. After all those years, Tremont and Gulf Railroad shut down there. Then it became necessary to move the rack or build a new one because Missouri & Pacific Railroad would not come in on the small track we had just off the main line. A new loading rack was built just down below the old warehouse [Arkansas Fuel Oil] in Tullos right off the Missouri & Pacific line. Then an eight-inch line was laid from the stock or treated tanks to the loading rack, about three hundred yards. All we had to do then was turn a tank on and oil would gravity there about 500 barrels an hour.

— Claude L. Gibson, 1994

The racks looked alike, except when they didn't.

A word about the loading rack at Urania. Everything on the rack was similar to the one at Denkman and at Tullos. We pumped oil from across the highway. We usually loaded only two or three cars a week there. This rack was on the left side of old Highway 165 [now LA 125], across the road from Harter Oil Company. I usually operated this rack as it took only three or four hours once a week. I might mention a thing or two about the oil from the Georgetown field. This oil was pumped through a four-inch line from the field to the Denkman loading rack with steam pumps. . . . Steam was generated by a boiler fired with oil, then turned on to a steam pump, which pumped the oil. This eliminated a motor. . . . Also, in Tullos behind old Selma Motor Company and Stella's Café, Hunt Oil had a loading rack close to Missouri & Pacific Railroad. Grady Holmes and Clarence Sanders worked this rack. Everything was similar to ours.

— Claude L. Gibson, 1994

Use of loading racks was discontinued in the late 1950s, and racks were dismantled. Tanker trucks took over the job, and they still move Tullos-Urania oil today. Olla's oil was always trucked. Unlike Tullos-Urania, which straddled the railroad, Olla's field lay several miles east of the rail line, logistically favoring the use of trucks.

CHAPTER 12

Hardhats

Since 1925, companies—big and small—and an occasional entrepreneur have tried their luck at Tullos-Urania and Olla. The story of their ventures invariably follows the same cycle of initial success-later decline/big outfits downsizing-little boys rising. So goes the oil field, everywhere. Some go boom, some go "bust."

Big Boys

Arkansas Fuel Oil-Cities Service Company

Born in Arkansas, Arkansas Fuel Oil started its Tullos-Urania operations by buying out Louisiana Oil & Refining Company. In February 1926, Louisiana Oil drilled its first Tullos well, the W. T. Bass No. 2 (Serial No. 9291), a ten-barrel a day producer (Fisk 1938, pl. 13). This was followed in June by the Tremont Lumber Company No. A-7 (Serial No. 9704), which made saltwater. Its Tremont Lumber Company No. B-17 (Serial No. 9273) punched into pay sand in late February 1927, raining 1,800 barrels of crude a day on the location but quickly played out and was plugged and abandoned a short time later (SONRIS 2000). No compliance reports were ever filed. Two dusters were drilled in 1930, the Urania No. F-5 (Serial No. 13140), which was completed as an Arkansas Fuel Oil well in May, and the Louisiana Central O & G No. 2 (Serial No. 13781), completed a month later under the old name, Louisiana Oil & Refining (Fisk 1938, pl. 13). Tremont A-7 and Louisiana Central O & G were completed in a timely fashion, within a month after being permitted. But the deep Urania No. F-5—it went to 6,432 feet—was spudded on July 1, 1929, eight and a half months *before* being permitted, and its initial status was not filed until ten months after spudding. Also irregular was the timing of the Bass well's initial status filing, over a year after drilling began. So were the delinquent compliance filings for Tremont B-17 (SONRIS 2000).

Louisiana Oil & Refining Company was struggling to stay afloat. Three out of its first four holes were dry and plugged and another clogged up within a week after finding oil. It couldn't pay for oil it had contracted to buy, and facing a lawsuit, it filed for bankruptcy in 1935.[1] Arkansas Fuel Oil Company assumed Louisiana Oil & Refining Company's holdings and debts, a rather backdoor debut for a fledgling company on its way to cornering a major share of Tullos-Urania's production.

Arkansas and its issue Cities Service drilled several wells over the next fifty years, twenty-three in Tullos-Urania and thirty-four in Olla (SONRIS 2000), which is not a lot considering that more than 4,000 holes puncture the terrain. Its last Olla well, the Mathews A-5 (Serial No. 153371), was permitted in September 1976; its last Tullos well, the Tremont Lumber Company C (Serial No. 990333) was completed

Well sits plugged and abandoned on Tullos Heirs Lease, Tullos. (Photograph by Jon Gibson)

in May 1971. But the company put a lot of oil in its pipelines by gobbling up producing leases and restoring old depleted wells. During the period between 1948 and 1959, for instance, Arkansas Pipeline Company handled an estimated 18,000-30,000 barrels of oil a month (Claude L. Gibson, pers. comm. 1994). It also ran Loe Oil Company's production. Placid handled as much as Arkansas did, maybe more.

Arkansas Fuel Oil built a warehouse on LA 125 about a half-mile south of downtown Tullos. Pipe was racked alongside, and behind the warehouse was the treating plant and newest loading rack, put up after Tremont and Gulf Railroad went out of business and Missouri-Pacific refused to pick up tank cars from its old Denkman loading rack in Rochelle. A row of company houses for the superintendent and other titled men was strung out along the road heading toward downtown. Employees and their families staged Christmas parties, square dances, and other festive events in the company's clubhouse, located downtown, north of the depot, and company barbeques were held at its picnic grounds on the M lease near New Union Church, north of town.

Faint echoes of laughter and pungent smells of barbeque drift on gentle breezes from Arkansas Fuel Oil picnic grounds, M Lease, Tullos in 2006. (Photograph by Michael Tradewell)

Arkansas was a busy outfit during the 1930s, 1940s, and 1950s. It had lots of hands, paid them well, and gave them good benefits. Employees became a close-knit bunch, almost like a big extended family. Times were good and Tullos, a busy place, though it never really shed its "rough and tumble" image, earned during the boom—it remained the only "wet" town in the parish.

But the inevitable caught up with it. Production flagged steadily, even with minor technological revivals afforded by gravel-packing and frequent well workovers (Fisk 1938, 188; SONRIS 2000). Insulated by miles, social circles, and field experience, corporate decision-makers—headquartered in Shreveport and Tulsa—looked at their balance sheets and started selling leases and transferring hands to other fields. This move broke up the Tullos gang. With the handwriting on the wall, Arkansas seized the opportunity and sold out to Cities Service in 1961—ending a three-decade run in Tullos. Cities Service held out a little longer in Tullos and even longer in Olla, but in the end, it too succumbed to profit margin, government regulations, and low reservoir potential.

In an effort to bolster cash flow, Cities Service started farming out its low producing leases in the late 1960s.

> *Normally what that means [is that] Cities Service would take a little bit of the override, you know, royalty . . . and we'd [M & M Oil Company] have an obligation to drill it [the lease]. . . . Well, we did that on the Cockerham lease in the Olla field. . . . We made a good well, in fact, it made eighty barrels a day, and that was the field allowable.*
> —Max W. Maxwell, 1994

Cities Service also saw the saltwater disposal laws as a threat to its survival. Up to this time, saltwater from the wells had just been allowed to run out on the ground. Castor Creek was poisoned, and the land was scalded and barren or dotted here and there with clumps of goatweed or baccharis. The disposal law ended all that. Both Cities Service and Placid argued with the state that they couldn't pay for putting saltwater back in the ground and bear the expense of running the wells too (Max W. Maxwell, pers. comm. 1994). When verbal argument didn't work, some opponents began showing up in Baton Rouge to try a different kind of persuasion.

It was not uncommon to see oil men with bulging back pockets and handshakes lined with hundred dollar bills openly roaming the floor of the senate chamber.

But being too costly to put saltwater back in the ground was *"a fallacy"* (Max W. Maxwell, pers. comm. 1994).

> *What we did, we went to an old well — still had the casing in it [and] the well wasn't producing and we didn't think we could work it over — and we had Loe Pipeyard come in and shoot holes in the casing at a zone, structural level, sand that would take the water. . . . We would tie in as many as five to eight producing wells to one disposal well.*
>
> — Max W. Maxwell, 1994

Cities Service and Placid started shutting down wells, and M & M and Loe Oil started buying them.

> *We [M & M Oil Company] bought this lease from Cities Service, . . . down on Little River. . . . Cities Service gave it up because the conservation department was going to make them raise their saltwater pits to where [they] wouldn't overflow. . . . They [Cities Service] didn't make any money the year before, . . . and Frayne knew what was down there in the sand. They were top-notch leases, I mean! They had glass pipes . . . that came in from*

Where the wild Baccharis grows, saltwater-scalded flat on M lease, Tullos. (Photograph by Jon Gibson)

From the Earth it came, to the Earth it returns. Saltwater disposal well, Tullos Heirs Lease, Tullos. (Photograph by Jon Gibson)

eight wells to a tank battery . . . and you could look through it and see how much color it [the oil] had in it. . . . They were just phenomenal. We paid $25,000 for this lease, and the first month, we shipped over $5,000 worth [of oil]. I showed [the shipping ticket] to old man Odum, who was the head of Louisiana Bank and Trust and he said: "Gawd damn, Maxwell, you'd like to make a deal like that everday, wudden' you?"

—Max W. Maxwell, 1994

Actually, the sell-off had been looming years earlier with production decline and Cities Service's costly offshore explorations. The company needed to accumulate big reserves to stay competitive, and Tullos just didn't have big reserves. Another bitter pill finally caught up with it—an aging infrastructure. Over the years, storms blew down a lot of the old wooden derricks, and back in the 1930s with oil selling for as low as a quarter a barrel, the wells were not put back in service. They simply weren't profitable at that price. Coupled with the good wages it was paying its hands—always more than other employers—Cities Service faced dark days ahead (Max W. Maxwell, pers. comm. 1994).

And the darkness finally came in 1982 when T. Boone Pickens, owner of Mesa Petroleum Company, attempted a hostile take-over. That bid was averted by a merger arrangement with Gulf Oil Corporation. However, the deal with Gulf fell apart, and Cities Service wound up merging with Occidental Petroleum Corporation, who promptly sold off the refining and retail divisions to Southland Corporation, owner of the 7-Eleven chain. In 1990, Southland sold them to Victor Chavez of Petroleos de Venezuela (Claude Gibson, pers. comm., 1994).

Arkansas Fuel Oil had come full circle. Born in a take-over, it died in one.

H. L. Hunt, Inc.-Placid Oil Company

In 1921, Haroldson Lafayette Hunt Jr. left the cotton fields of eastern Arkansas headed for El Dorado where a booming oil field had just come in (Anonymous 1996b, 10; Franks and Lambert 1982, 107-122). With only fifty dollars to his name, he jumped into lease brokering and, six months later, sunk his first well, the Hunt-Pickering No. 1, with an old rig he acquired by paying the holding and freight charges (Anonymous 1996b, 10). After drilling a few more wells at El Dorado and buying leases in the nearby Smackover field, Hunt decided to incorporate, and on December 28, 1925, he officially became H. L. Hunt, Inc. The new company name carried until December 14, 1935, when it was changed to Placid Oil Company in order to avoid tax increases slated to take effect in 1936. He deftly implemented the maneuver by establishing trusts for his six children (mothered by Lyda Bunker Hunt) and funding them with shares of Placid stock (Brown 1976, 91, 142; Robert Gray, William Davis, and Delbert Noble, pers. comm. 1983).

Whether prophetic or not, incorporation came just five days before Hunt purchased the Tullos Heirs lease, which now harbors several of the oldest-producing wells in the Tullos-Urania field.

> The lease during the first year [1926] produced approximately 1,700 barrels per day of 21° gravity oil . . . run in earthen storage [open lease pits], then treated. It was transported by H. L. Hunt tank cars. Later this year, a pipeline and loading rack was put into operation. . . . For many years, Mr. Hunt controlled approximately 20 percent of the production from this area.
> — Robert Gray, William Davis, and Delbert Noble, 1983

In 1928, Hunt bought out three small companies, Catalina Oil Company, Pima Oil Company, and Arizola Petroleum Company (Robert Gray, William Davis, and Delbert Noble, pers. comm. 1983). Together with leases he acquired from Urania Lumber Company and individuals, he was producing thirteen leases in the Tullos-Urania field. Expansion necessitated new facilities, and by year's end, he built the Urania A treating plant, the Urania loading rack, and the Tullos water works. In 1929, he constructed a company warehouse in Tullos (Robert Gray, William Davis, Delbert Noble, pers. comm. 1983), just across the road (LA 125) from the treating plant.

As drilling slowed in Tullos-Urania in the 1930s—only sixty-three permits were issued during the decade (SONRIS 2000)—the price of oil also dropped. Prices fell from a nationwide average of $1.19 a barrel in 1930 to $0.65 in 1931 (they were a rock-bottom $0.10 a barrel for East Texas oil). Hunt focused on production in Tullos-Urania and on leasing and exploration in surrounding parts of the parish, as well as in the huge East Texas field (Anonymous 1996b, 10-11; Robert Gray, William Davis, and Delbert Noble, pers. comm. 1983). In January 1936, Hunt leased over 60,000 acres from

Louisiana Central Lumber Company, most of which (over 56,000 acres, or 92 percent) was in LaSalle Parish.

In 1940, his newly restructured company Placid, which he still ruled though technically it belonged to his children, brought in the prolific Olla field on the Louisiana Central lease, and rapidly thereafter, Placid discovered the Little Creek and Nebo fields. Since then, Placid has developed over a dozen new fields in central Louisiana (Baldwin et al. 2007; Robert Gray, William Davis, and Delbert Noble, pers. comm. 1983).

From 1926 on, Hunt-Placid continuously has taken more oil out

On location in Olla field, H. L. Hunt in suit (left) and James Justiss in work clothes, 1941. (Courtesy of Jennifer Loe, Justiss Oil Company)

of the ground in and around Tullos-Urania and Olla than any other company. Its presence has not only stimulated the local economy, but, even scaled-down, it has been the financial backbone since the lumber mills pulled out. It's nearly impossible to talk about the old days of the Tullos-Urania and Olla fields without talking to a Placid working-man or retiree. The legacy of H. L. Hunt is as ever-lasting as the river of oil running beneath the pines.

Justiss-Mears Oil Company/Justiss Oil Company

In 1946, James Fowler "Jick" Justiss teamed up with Carroll G. Mears to create the Justiss-Mears Partnership—later corporation (Anonymous 1996a, 5). Justiss, a former muleskinner in Smackover, Arkansas, was the "nuts and bolts" of the outfit and Mears was the financial arranger. Justiss had broken into the field as a roustabout for H. L. Hunt during the Tullos boom and within months was running Hunt's Tullos-Urania operations, gaining Hunt's confidence with his unerring ability to meet Hunt's shipping goals (Anonymous 1996a, 5).

> Mr. Hunt didn't think I could ship that much oil out of Tullos [500 tank cars per month] and still stay within the spending budget he gave me. But I fooled him. The first month I hit my shipping target right on the button and I ran over my spending budget by only $100. Even Mr. Hunt, who seldom gave out a compliment, said that wasn't bad. I told him I'd do better next month. And I did. I came within $50 of my spending budget the second month. When I told Mr. Hunt, he said that I seemed to understand the oil business and should use my own judgment about spending from then on. I never forgot that lesson.
> —James F. Justiss, 1996 (Anonymous 1996a, 5)

While still with Hunt (then corporately reorganized as Placid Oil Company), Justiss led the opening of the Olla field, followed quickly by discoveries of other LaSalle Parish fields (Anonymous 1996a, 5-6). Energized by his Wilcox wildcatting successes, he amicably left Hunt's employ and with Mears started a drilling partnership in 1946 (Anonymous 1996a, 6). They purchased a drilling rig on credit and picked up two wells in the Olla field, the A. J. Ward A-1 (Serial No. 26219) and the Jones A-1 (probably Serial No. 26663).

The A. J. Ward well and lease were a steal—purchase price of

James Justiss (right) and buddy inspect motor on A. J. Ward A-1, Olla in 1946. (Courtesy of Jennifer Loe, Justiss Oil Company)

$400! The well was dead and lacked an access road, but Justiss laid a board road and a pipeline, reworked the well, and restored production to fifty barrels of oil a day *"for nearly twenty-five years"* (Anonymous 1996a, 6). The producing Jones well cost $20,000, but it was a steal too. It was making a hundred barrels a day, and despite the rock-bottom price of oil, a buck eighty a barrel, the well paid out in just over a hundred days.

Justiss-Mears was up and running. Reorganization and

expansion soon carried the Justiss Oil Company well beyond its humble beginnings in the Olla field and transformed it into one of the country's premier drilling outfits (Anonymous 1996a, 7-10), a fitting legacy for an old boy, nicknamed Jick, who broke-in roustabouting in Tullos with dreams of drilling oil wells!

Little Boys

Loe Oil Company

Loe Oil Company was one of Tullos's longest continually operating independents. Brothers Glen and Bert came in on the heels of Tullos's boom, and Glen's son, Shelby, is following in their footsteps. His company, S. H. Loe Oil Corp., is the biggest operator in Tullos today, pumping more than 300 wells (SONRIS 2000).

> *Bert came to Tullos working as a pumper for H. L. Hunt in the Olla field. . . , probably sometime in the mid-1940s, perhaps as late as '47. Then, apparently independent of or with his brother Glen, later, about '47 or '49 or sometime in that vicinity, they purchased, or Bert purchased, a casing company, and began to run casing. . . . Not only was his work confined to Tullos, but he worked elsewhere, particularly in South Texas. . . . Led him to believe that he could get a few of those wells and produce them himself. . . . Began to buy some wells and this was the birth of the Loe Oil Company*
> —M. W. Fife Jr. (pers. comm. 1994)

> *Loe Oil Company began operating a [second-hand] pipeyard. . . . First got in the oil business by buying some of Arkansas Fuel Oil's wells — some of these wells were pretty good ones. . . . The Loes got their start by borrowing money to buy and drill wells. . . . [They were] still operating*

Loe Oil Company sign shows its age in 2011. (Photograph by Jon Gibson)

*their pipeyard — they sold pipe and second-hand pumping units. They did
pretty well, I think.*

—Claude L. Gibson, 1994

M & M Oil Company

Max W. Maxwell and Frayne Miles got into the business in the
1960s, long after the drilling peak was over. Their collaboration
worked because: *"Frayne took care of the oil field, I took care of . . . the
money, . . . borrowing money and getting leases, things like that"* (Max
W. Maxwell, pers. comm. 1994).

> *He [Frayne Miles] and I were . . . with Woodman [Woodman of the World
> Life Insurance Company]. So he borrowed $3,000 on his renewals, and I
> borrowed $5,000 from the insurance, and we drilled a well. That was real
> poor boys doing it — scrounging materials. We made a well, . . . and that's
> the one we called Betty. It was a good well. In fact, it made twelve barrels
> a day, which was big production at that time for Tullos. We mortgaged
> that well to the bank . . . for $10,000 and drilled another well, and we made
> another well. And on that same twenty acres, we made the third well that
> way, and the fourth well was dry.*
>
> *Let's see, . . . we wound up with nineteen [wells]. That was in 1967. . . . We
> started picking up leases. We started in 1971 . . . with thirty-two of those
> little wells in Tullos, on top of the Wilcox . . . , and we sold them to Earl
> Harter, Harter Oil Company, for $290,000, and, of course, we thought that
> was all the money there was in the world.*

—Max W. Maxwell, 1994

Old Boys

Scores of other operators have come and gone since 1925. Many
made money, many lost it. Yet, whether lost playing Five-Card
Stud, shooting craps, or drilling dry holes or made by drilling
fourteen producers in a row, patenting a new piece of equipment,
or simply working long and hard, Tullos-Urania and Olla hardhats
had their day in the sun and the mud.

CHAPTER 13

Good to the Last Drop

That Old Firefly Magic

Oil still flows through Olla and Tullos's veins, although the monetary potency of the syrupy black elixir has diminished. Commercial Olla has been on the downturn since the drilling fall-off in the mid-1940s (Elliot 1995, 26; Winberry 1995, 30-33). Unlike Tullos, the oil field and the corporate limits of Olla were never coextensive. You could go to the Post Office without hearing the rapid bark of a pumper or cross Main Street without waiting on a workover unit to pass. You had to go three miles southeast of town to enter Olla's oil kingdom. Unlike Tullos, Olla always had more stores, more merchandise, more services, and more consumers drawn from a wider hinterland. Unlike Tullos, Olla was not totally wound around the volatility of oil's fortunes. You can still buy groceries and get a haircut and a frosted coke in Olla. And kids still run for school buses at the three o'clock bell. Olla hangs on by the sheer doggedness of its residents and is even experiencing modest revitalization through downtown renewal, music festivals, and cultural-historical celebrations.

Some of the young people who grew up here during the fifties have said, "I wish it was like it used to be here when we could buy anything we wanted right here in this town when business boomed. Remember the fireflies in summer." It has something to do with the fact that they hardly ever see a firefly now. But when they do, they say they are tempted to catch it, trap it in a bottle, and save it for morning. But they never do. They say they just don't want to spoil the magic. (Winberry 1995, 33)

Olla's main street deserted in the summer of 1994. "We need better jobs and better working conditions," they say. "I'd leave here, but I'm not a quitter," said another young person (Winberry 1995, 33). (Photograph by Jon Gibson)

Yet, that old firefly magic runs deep. Just ask the "old-timers" who gather around the burning barrel at the Burger Barn on frosty mornings why they stay in Olla. To a man, they will tell you that they were born and raised in Olla, as were their people before them, and that they want to be laid to rest here in Chickasaw Paradise when the Good Lord calls.

In 1950, 732 people lived in Tullos (Louisiana Almanac 1969, 92-94). By 1960, 138 souls, or nearly 20 percent, had either died or left town, most being transferred by downsizing oil companies. Downtown businesses began closing their doors, never to be opened again. By the '70s, old downtown nearly was deserted, left were only boarded-up buildings to stare at the occasional post-office patron and Sunday church-goer.

When Ghosts Gather

Today, only about 375 souls call Tullos home, down from its storied peak of 10,000. They shop at the Jena Wal-Mart and attend school in Urania and Olla. The old store buildings are gone now, but mail is still posted at 71479, refrains of "Amazing Grace" drift from the First Baptist Church on Sundays, the dearly departed

"On one side of Main Street, vines crawl over piles of concrete blocks and weeds poke up through cracks in old foundations being ground slowly and surely into dust by the mighty hand of time. On the other side of the street, old brick store fronts long ago shut their dark window eyes unable to watch. Yet, every now and then, crumbling walls and rubble heaps sigh and whisper like gentle breezes." (Gibson 1999, 12). (Photograph by Michael Tradewell)

find eternal peace in Magnolia and New Union cemeteries, and the thirsty can always find a cold beer. And at dusk, when ghosts gather in old downtown, gentle stirrings still intone Frenchy Robichaux's words from the floor of old No. 6: "Better take cover, boys, 'cause she's fixing to blow."

Acknowledgments

A bunch of fine folks, living and departed, helped out with this book, and I am much obliged to: Bob L. Allbritton; Jesse E. Albritton; Madge Bailey; Maple Tyler Book; Gerald J. Brady; Lorraine Tisdale Byrd; Luther Byrd; Lane Capps; E. Forrest Cook; William Davis; Terry Dobbins; Kevin Dockery; John Lee "Junior" Doughty, Jr.; Clara Belle Gibson Evans; Erin Gibson Faherty; M. W. "Mac" Fife, Sr.; M. W. Fife, Jr.; Mike Ganey; Claude L. Gibson; Mary Beth Sellers Gibson; Eugene Goodwin; Jimmy Roy Goodwin; Robert Gray; Carla Hallmark; Doug Hallmark; Jerry Harris; Joe Hargrove; Bobby Harter; Paul Heinrich; Tom Henslee; Brad Hodges; W. L. Holmes; Robert "Nip" Ivy; James "Jick" Justiss; Melba King; Sonny King; Jennifer Justiss Loe; Shelby H. Loe; Bob Lurry; Rene Evans Lurry; Max W. Maxwell; Richard McCulloh; W. C. "Willie" McDaniels; Daphne Gibson McLeod; Ferndale Allbritton McKeithen; Glen Dale McKeithen; Robin Moody; William Earl Moody; Delbert Noble; E. W. Nugent; Huey "Petey" Randall; Judith A. Schiebout; Thomas M. Sessions; Martha Huffman Smith; Gary Stringer; Michael Tradewell; Robert Wagner, Jr.; G. Aubra Wall; Juanita Fife Wall; and J. S. "Buddy" Williams.

Notes

Preface

1. Interviews recorded in 1983 by Juanita Fife Wall and in 1994 by me. Wall interviewed William Davis (Placid retiree, deceased); M. W. Fife, Sr. (Placid retiree, deceased); Robert Gray (Placid retiree, deceased); Joe Hargrove (Placid retiree, deceased); W. L. Holmes (Placid retiree, deceased); James Justiss (owner of Justiss Oil Company); Delbert Noble (Placid retiree, deceased); Robert Wagner, Jr. (Placid retiree, deceased); and G. A. Wall (Arkansas Fuel Oil retiree, deceased). Juanita donated her research notes to me in 1998. I recorded conversations with Clara Belle Evans (co-owner of Sam Evans Grocery, Tullos, deceased); Norris Davis (Arkansas Fuel Oil/Cities Service retiree, deceased); M. W. Fife, Jr. (S. H. Loe Oil Company retiree); Claude L. Gibson (Arkansas Pipeline/Cities Service retiree, deceased); Max W. Maxwell (co-owner with Frayne Miles of M & M Oil Company, deceased); and W. C. McDaniels (Placid retiree, deceased). Tapes of recorded interviews with Evans, Davis, Gibson, Hargrove, Maxwell, and McDaniels are curated at the Centennial Cultural Center, in Olla, Louisiana.

Chapter 2

1. Residual gravity mapping dampens this possibility. J. D. Rogers suggests that the salt, instead, comes from brine leaks escaping from the Cockfield aquifer along faults radiating upward through the capping Vicksburg-Jackson formations (Echols and McCulloh 2004, 4).

2. SONRIS stands for Strategic Online Natural Resources Information System.

3. A machine shop (bit shop) is a smithy or blacksmith where drill bits and oil field tools were repaired.

4. Spud dates are not given for the remaining wildcat wells, and Fisk's Nos. L-24 and L-30 are the same well. This accounts for the discrepancies between Fisk's numbers and the author's.

Chapter 3

1. Joe Hargrove quote from an interview with Juanita Fife Wall on February 22, 1983 regarding the George Zeigen et al. Urania Lumber Company No. 1

Chapter 4

1. Hargrove was right the first time. The Goodwin-Daniels well came in on

February 6, 1926, and the Hardtner, Edenborn & Collins well was not spudded until November 15, 1926 (SONRIS 2000).

Chapter 5

1. W. C. McDaniels quote from an interview with the author on July 6, 1994.

2. Lane Capps informed the author that one of his relatives told him that this particular building served as the Masonic lodge. Masons may have met here later, but based on the number of small rooms facing each other across a long hallway, the building seems to have started out as a boarding house.

3. Another version of the same story claims that patrons downstairs "heard some women hollering for help in one of the houses," i.e., whorehouses or barrelhouses (Williams 1976, 6). Joe Hargrove shared a similar story in a 1976 interview with Cecil Williams. The versions may not be mutually exclusive.

Chapter 8

1. API stands for the American Petroleum Institute, which is the national trade organization that represents the United States' oil and natural gas industry.

2. Minor production comes from the overlying Sparta formation.

3. While a catastrophic collision with an asteroid (or comet, says other astronomers) often is blamed for the extinction of the dinosaurs, other theories abound; a sampling—widespread volcanism spawning disastrous global cooling; spreading virulent diseases into virgin-soil populations by climate change-prompted mass migrations; and colder climate producing unisex reptilian populations and reduced fecundity (Wallace 1987, 108-119). Doubters persist, and the final word on the matter remains to be spoken (Colbert 1983).

4. Geologist Gary Stringer is an authority on fossil fish-ear bones (otoliths), especially of Eocene species. Dr. Stringer recently received the high honor of having a fossil fish named after him, *Pogonias stringeri*.

Chapter 9

1. In later wells, holes were shot through the casing walls with steel bullets electronically fired from a flat metal bar lowered downhole into the production zone. These bullets perforated the casing allowing fluid to come in.

2. Today's drilling mud is a mixture of clay, water, and chemicals pumped down the well through the drill pipe. Not only does mud cool bits, suppress pressure, and lubricate pipe, but it carries downhole cuttings to the surface, fills in the annulus preventing it from caving in, and keeps unwanted fluids from entering the borehole.

Chapter 10

1. Max Maxwell (per. comm. 1994) noted that Cities Service was making around two barrels a day per well at the time (1971-72), so getting four barrels was good production for Tullos.

Chapter 11

1. Tullos's "green oil" is really black oil, or crude with an asphalt base. Green oil, by definition, has a paraffin base (Langekamp 2006, 188).

Chapter 12

1. The lawsuit—the case of Arkansas Fuel Oil Co. v. Louisiana ex rel. Muslow, 304 U.S. 197—went all the way to the U.S. Supreme Court and was decided in 1938.

Oil Field Vernacular: Glossary

annulus—Space between well casing and walls of borehole.

backed off—Joint of pipe or sucker rod that becomes unscrewed in the borehole.

bail—The heavy arcuate handle of a swivel that fits over the big hook while drilling; also the act of cleaning out the borehole with a bailer.

bailer—Sleeve-like metal container used to dip mud and cuttings from the borehole.

bit shop—A machine shop where oil-field tools and equipment were repaired, sometimes on a forge.

blowout—Uncontrolled escape of gas and fluid from the borehole; see gusher.

blowing hole—An erupting well; see blowout.

boll weevil—An inexperienced drilling rig worker; a convenient scapegoat for mistakes around the rig; also, called a worm.

BOP—Blowout preventer; a heavy-duty valve assembly connected to well casinghead in order to prevent uncontrolled discharge of gas and fluid from the production sand.

breadbasket—Traveling block, swivel, elevators, and big hook assembly used to raise and lower pipe and rods in the well borehole.

breaking out joints—Unscrewing drill pipe or casing at threaded connections.

bridle—A cable fitting, which connects the well end of a walking beam to the well's polished rod; equitably distributes the beam's pulling force and maintains the proper alignment between the arcuate swinging motion of the beam and vertical up-and-down movement of the polished rod.

BS&W—Acronym for basic sediment and water, impurities normally present in crude oil.

cable tool drilling—Early method of drilling whereby a heavy, chisel-edged bit was repeatedly raised and dropped by a steam-driven walking beam, thereby pounding a hole into the earth.

cap—Sealing off an abandoned well by pouring mud and cement down the borehole in order to prevent gas and oil from reaching the surface or from flowing into other downhole strata.

casing—Outermost pipe string run into a well's borehole in order to prevent saltwater intrusion and collapse of the hole.

casinghead gas—Natural gas produced by an oil well, as opposed to a gas well.

central power—Assembly used to pump multiple wells at once; shackle lines tied a group of surrounding wells to a large, steam-driven, flat-lying bandwheel, which turned eccentrically departing an alternating push-pull motion to the lines and, in turn, a reciprocating up-down motion to the walking beams of the wells' pumping units.

couple—Screwing together two joints of threaded pipe; see uncouple.

crown block—Fixed pulley system at the top of a derrick used to raise and lower a pipe or rods in the hole.

derrick—Standing wooden or, later, steel tower used as a fulcrum for drilling and workover operations; replaced in later times by a pop-up mast mounted on a mobile drilling or pulling unit.

derrickman—Roughneck who racks the pipe or rods pulled from the borehole while perched on a monkey board in the derrick.

disposal well—Used to eliminate saltwater by pumping it into a stratigraphically sealed-off formation.

drawworks—The powered hoisting assembly on the floor of a drilling rig, which includes the bull wheel, or hoisting drum, cables, clutches, brakes, and power take-off. The driller "drives" the drawworks, thereby drilling the well.

drill collar—Heavy, thick-walled piece of pipe connecting drill bit with drill pipe, which added weight and strength at the point of maximum drilling stress.

drill string—Run of made-up joints of pipe and attached bit used to drill the borehole.

dog house—Portable, single-room shed set up on location used for tool and supply storage, shelter, and changing clothes.

dry hole—Well that failed to strike oil.

duster—See dry hole.

eight-up oil wagon—Mule- or ox-drawn wooden vehicle used for hauling heavy loads of pipe, equipment, and lumber; eight-up wagon had eight wheels and a four-up wagon had four wheels; number of draft animals harnessed ranged from four to ten, sometimes even more, depending on how heavy the load and how deep the mire; also, four-up oil wagon.

farm out—Business arrangement whereby a lease holder permits another outfit to drill on the leased area for a share of the profit.

fireman—Nervous worker who fired the boiler on old steam rigs.

firing boilers—Keeping boilers supplied with sufficient wood, gas, or water needed to pressurize the steam engine that powered the drilling.

flathead—Vernacular name for a lumber company worker who saws down trees. It humorously envisions the case of an awkwardly fallen tree landing on the head of the sawyer and mashing it flat.

going fishing—Retrieving objects broken off or dropped into the casing using specialized tools lowered from the rig floor.

gone in the hole—Rigger or derrickman killed in a fall from the derrick; more generally, the death of a hardhat.

gusher—Wild well that comes in with so much gas pressure that a plume of oil is forced up the derrick.

hand—Worker on a drilling, workover, or pipeline crew.

hardhat—Roughneck or roustabout who wears a protective aluminum or hard plastic hat.

hard nose—End of a walking beam connected to the Pittman arm, opposite the end connected to well's polished rod.

headache post—Timber frame built on well floor underneath heavy wooden walking beam to keep it from falling on roughnecks when being disconnected from the Pittman arm.

heads—Oil that flows in spurts; intermittent flow of oil.

horsehead—Horsehead-shaped metal fixture mounted on the end of a steel walking beam opposite the hard nose; holds the mounting guides for a loop of cable, called the bridle, which attaches to the well's rod string and pulls it up and down, thereby pumping the well.

Kelly joint—The first and strongest joint of the drill string. Unlike regular cylindrical pipe, the joint has flatten sides, which snuggly fit into the square hole in the rotary table enabling it to spin with the engine-powered rotary.

making up joints — Screwing together two pieces of threaded pipe with a large wrench or tongs.

monkey board — Several two-by-eight boards laid side-by-side across the derrick girts where the derrickman stands when maneuvering tubing or sucker rods from the pipe stand to the floor hands during completing or pulling a well.

mud-eater — Person who examines (tastes) well cuttings or cores in an effort to identify pay sand.

mud hose — Pliable reinforced tube used to carry drilling mud from the mud pit down into the drill pipe and back up the annulus.

offset — Well drilled next to an earlier well, which encountered shows of oil but, for one reason or another, could not be completed; also, offsetting.

oil field dove — Prostitute.

oil sand — Porous, oil-bearing sedimentary stratum.

parted rods — Broken or unscrewed sucker rod string.

pay sand — Underground oil-producing zone.

plugging a well — Filling casing of no-longer producing well with mud and cement to prevent the escape of oil and gas; see cap.

pulling a well — Removing sucker-rod string from well casing in order to service or replace downhole pump; also, lifting rods to find and replace a broken connection in the rod string itself; also, pulling rods.

pulling doubles — Removing pipe or rods from downhole after unscrewing every other joint.

pulling tribbles — Removing pipe or rods from downhole three connected joints at a time.

pumping barrel — Part of a well's downhole pump, which fills with crude from the producing sand when the piston, or traveling barrel, is withdrawn by the upward motion of the surface pump's walking beam; on the ensuing downstroke, the traveling barrel once again plunges into the stationary, fluid-filled barrel (standing valve) at the bottom of the well lifting the oil up the tubing toward the surface.

proved — A location where oil has been discovered and determined to be recoverable, usually by wildcatting.

rat hole — Slanted, pipe-lined hole dug near a well's borehole where the Kelly joint is placed when not actively engaged in drilling.

rosinbelly — Lumber company employee who works in a sawmill; name applies to sawyers, planers, and stackers who handle green pine lumber directly thereby smearing rosin on their bellies.

roughneck—Hands on the drilling crew; beside the driller, early rigs normally were manned by two floor hands, a derrickman, and a fireman.

roughnecking—Carrying out all jobs required to drill an oil well from rigging up the drilling equipment, through drilling and completing the well to dismantling the equipment.

roustabout—Oil field workers who service and repair existing wells, put up tanks, lay pipelines, and generally carry out all other labor involved in moving oil from well to start of delivery to buyer; also, roustabouting.

rotary drilling—Boring a well hole with a spinning drill; generally replaced cable-tool drilling in the early twentieth century.

running oil—Piping oil from a tank to a delivery terminal.

sanded up—Well borehole choked with sand washed-in from the production zone.

shak-a-line—Shackle line; a long string of sucker rods connecting a pumping unit to a large, powered, flat-lying bandwheel, or central power; the wheel turned eccentrically and pulled the string back and forth, thereby driving the pumping unit; shak-a-lines were run to several wells, and the same power pumped them all at the same time.

shows of oil—In the early days, any sign of oil in samples taken from the borehole.

skidding a rig—Towing a standing derrick from one location to another nearby along a log roller-surmounted board road with winch truck or mule/ox team.

spudding a well—The start of drilling; initial penetration of the ground surface with the drill bit.

stabbing—Maneuvering the male end of a joint of pipe or casing into the female end of another joint in order to make a connection.

standard (drilling) rig—Basic cable-tool rig modified for rotary drilling in early twentieth century; steam-powered rotary table installed under wooden derrick spun the drill string, replacing old-time hoisted-and-dropped percussion bit.

standard (pumping) rig—Oil well pumped by steam-driven belt-bandwheel-walking beam assembly; engine and belt-bandwheel were enclosed in buildings and walking beam was set up under wooden derrick; up-and-down motion of walking beam pumped well.

standpipe—Vertical joint of pipe mounted under derrick, which carries drilling mud from mud pump through the mud hose and into the drill pipe.

standing valve—Stationary part of a well's downhole pump, which sucks in crude from the formation when the traveling barrel, or plunger, is withdrawn. When the traveling barrel plunges back into the refilled standing valve, it forces the fluid upward through the small void between the tubing and the sucker rods and is carried to the surface.

stuffing box—Short length of pipe connections attached to wellhead, through which the polished rod continually moves up and down; box is "stuffed" with packing to prevent fluid or gas leaks.

swivel—Heavy steel appliance suspended from the big hook, which allows the connected Kelly joint and drill string to spin without twisting the traveling block and hoisting lines.

tailing rods—In workover jobs, dragging an uncoupled sucker rod from the well casing and laying it on the ground outside the derrick; a good way to break-in green hands or remind worms of their stunts; also, tailing doubles, tailing tribbles.

tailing doubles—When tailing rods and two rods are left connected.

tailing tribbles—When tailing rods and three rods are left connected.

traveling valve—Component of well's downhole pump pulled up and down by the string of sucker rods.

tripping—Continually adding new joints of drill pipe or casing to downhole pipe string.

uncouple— Unscrewing two joints of threaded pipe; see couple.

wildcat—Risky exploratory well drilled outside a proved field.

wildcatter—An outfit or person who drills wells outside a proved field.

wildcatting—Drilling exploratory wells.

windjammer—Large natural gas-driven compressor that jettisoned air into the producing sand in an attempt to force oil up the casing.

working derricks—Job of the derrickman on a drilling crew; racking casing or tubing pulled from the well while balancing on a lofty perch (known as the monkey board) up in the derrick; not for hands with a fear of heights or with a hangover.

workover—Any number of jobs carried out by roustabouts to repair or improve production in a working well.

worm— An inexperienced hand or one prone to make mistakes.

Bibliography

"50 Years! Definitely Something to Celebrate!" *The Hard Hat* (Justiss Oil, Baker/ Altech, Jena, Louisiana) (June, July, August, September 1996): 3-9.

Baldwin, Bill, Margie Bowles, and Ellen Gunter. *Riding for the Brand: The Story of Hunt Petroleum Corporation and the Employees Who Fueled Its Success.* Dallas: Hunt Petroleum, 2007.

Beard, Sylvester Q., Jr., and Gary L. Stringer. "Paleoenvironment of a Diverse Marine Vertebrate Fauna from the Yazoo Clay (Late Eocene) at Copenhagen, Caldwell Parish, Louisiana." In *Transactions of the Gulf Coast Association of Geological Societies* (Copenhagen, LA: AAPG Bulletin, 1995) 45: 77-85.

Brown, Stanley H. *H. L. Hunt.* Chicago: Playboy Press, 1976.

Burns, Anna C. "The Forest Industry in LaSalle." In *Born and Raised on Castor Creek: A Century of Change*, by Jon L. Gibson, 37-41. Olla, LA: Louisiana Endowment for the Humanities, 1999.

Caplinger, Michael W. *Allegheny Oil Heritage Project: A Contextual Overview of Crude Oil Production in Pennsylvania.* Historic American Engineering Record No. PA-436. Morgantown, WV: Institute for the History of Technology and Industrial Archaeology, 1997.

Caraway, Octavia H. "Discovery of Oil Makes Tullos Boom Town Over Night." In *20's. Jena Times/Olla-Tullos Signal,* June 20, 1979.

Carpenter, Kenneth, and David White. "Feeding in the Archaeocete Whale. Zygorhiza kochii (Cetacea: Archaeoceti)." *Mississippi Geology* 7, no. 2 (1986), 1-14.

Clark, Cathy. "Oil Boom Spewed Life into Tullos." *News-Star-World*, May 22, 1983.

Colbert, Edwin H. *Dinosaurs: An Illustrated History.* Maplewood, NJ: Hammond, 1983.

Cook, E. Forrest, ed. Extracts from the Log of the Southern Camp, Urania, LA, n.d. Unpublished notes from student journals, Yale University School of Forestry in Urania. Journals on file, Town Hall, Urania, Louisiana.

Darrah, William C. *Pithole: The Vanished City.* Gettysburg: printed by author, 1972.

Dockery, David T., III, and Katie Lightsey. *Windows into Mississippi's Geologic Past.* Circular 6. Jackson: Mississippi Office of Geology, 1997.

Doughty, B. E. *The Scrapbook of a Detective.* Vol. 1. New York: Carlton Press, 1974.

Doughty, John L., Jr. "Why Junior Loves the Blues." *Junior's Juke Joint.* http://www.deltablues.net/tullos.html, 1996.

Echols, John B., and Richard P. McCulloh. "Little Creek Structure, T9N-R2E, LaSalle Parish, Louisiana." *Basin Research Institute Bulletin* 8 (1998): 30-39.

Elliott, James R. "'Oil, Timber, and Sulphur Water": The Early History of Olla, Louisiana." In *A History of the Town of Olla, 1830-1995*. Olla, Louisiana: privately printed, 1995.

Fisk, Harold N. "Geology of Grant and LaSalle Parishes." *Geological Bulletin No. 10*. New Orleans: Louisiana Geological Survey,1938.

Franks, Kenny A. *The Oklahoma Petroleum Industry*. Norman: University of Oklahoma Press, 1980.

Franks, Kenny A., and Paul F. Lambert. *Early Louisiana and Arkansas Oil, A Photographic History, 1901-1946*. College Station: Texas A & M University Press, 1982.

Franks, Kenny A., Paul F. Lambert, and Carl N. Tyson. *Early Oklahoma Oil, A Photographic History, 1859-1936*. College Station: Texas A & M University Press, 1981.

Gibson, Jon L. *Born and Raised on Castor Creek: A Century of Change*. Olla, LA: Louisiana Endowment for the Humanities, 1999.

Guinn, Jeff. *Go Down Together: The True, Untold Story of Bonnie & Clyde*. New York: Simon & Schuster, 2010.

Haque, Syed M. *Lignite Resources in Louisiana*. Public Information Series No. 5. Baton Rouge: Louisiana Geological Survey, 2000.

Harris, Gilbert D. "The Cretaceous and Lower Eocene Faunas of Louisiana. Special Report No. 6." *Geological Survey of Louisiana, Report for 1899*. Baton Rouge: Louisiana State University, 1899, 289-310.

Harris, Gilbert D., and A. C. Veatch. "General Geology." *Geological Survey of Louisiana, Report for 1899*. Baton Rouge: Louisiana State University, 1899, 45-138.

Hill, Margaret Hunt. *H.L. and Lyda*. Little Rock: August House, 1994.

Huner, J., Jr. "Geology of Caldwell and Winn Parishes." *Geological Bulletin No. 15*. New Orleans: Louisiana Geological Survey, 1939.

Hunt, Haroldson L. *Hunt Heritage*. Dallas: Parade Press, 1973.

Jena Times/Olla-Tullos Signal. "History of Oil in Parish Is Recalled," March 30, 1988.

Justiss Oil. *Justiss Oil Company, 50th Anniversary*. Jena: Justiss Oil, 1996.

Langenkamp, R. D. *Handbook of Oil Industry Terms & Phrases*. 5th ed. Tulsa: Penn Well, 2006.

Ley, Normand W., William R. Paine, Charles F. Levert, Jr., Charles C. Smith, John B. Tubb, and Paul F. Johnson. *Tertiary of Central Louisiana, October 3-4, 1968*. Lafayette: Lafayette Geological Society, 1968.

Louisiana Almanac. New Orleans: Pelican, 1969.

Lynch, Gerald. *Roughnecks, Drillers, and Tool Pushers: Thirty-Three Years in the Oil Fields*. Austin: University of Texas Press, 1987.

McCulloh, Richard P., and Lori G. Eversull. "Shale-Filled Channel System in the Wilcox Group (Paleocene-Eocene). North-Central South Louisiana." In *Continental Slope: Frontier of the '80s, Transactions of the 36th Annual Meeting of Gulf Coast Association of Geological Societies*, edited by Darwin Knochenmus, George Cardwell, and Fonda Lindfors-Kearns, 213-18. Baton Rouge: Gulf Coast Association of Geological Societies, 1986.

McPherson, A. Bradley, and Earl M. Manning. "New Records of Eocene Sea Snakes (*Pterosphenus*) from Louisiana." In *Montgomery Landing Site, Marine Eocene (Jackson) of Central Louisiana*, edited by Judith A. Schiebout and William van den Bold, 197-208. Baton Rouge: Thirty-Sixth Annual Meeting of the Gulf Coast Association of Geological Societies, 1986.

"Men of Tullos-Urania." *Pay Sand* 4, no. 4 (1945): 1, 4-5.

Missouri Pacific Railroad: The First 125 Years. Privately printed, n.d.

Mott, H. J. (recorder). Minutes of Conferences, Tullos First Baptist Church, February 2, 6, and 13, and August 8, 1935. Unpublished records, on file, Tullos First Baptist Church, Tullos, Louisiana.

Nolf, D., and Gary Stringer. "Late Eocene (Priabonian) Fish Otoliths from the Yazoo Clay at Copenhagen, Louisiana." *Geological Pamphlet No. 13.* Baton Rouge: Louisiana Geological Survey, 2003.

Nunn, Lori L. "Forminiferal Biostratigraphy and Paleoecology of the Wilcox Group (Paleocene-Eocene) in Central and Southern Louisiana." In *Continental Slope: Frontier of the '80s,* edited by Darwin Knochenmus, George Cardwell, and Fonda Lindfors-Kearns, 511-16. *Transactions Vol. 36.* Baton Rouge: Gulf Coast Association of Geological Societies, 1986.

"Oil Fields." *Pay Sand* 21, no. 1 (1996): 10-12.

Oil Weekly. Houston: Gulf, 1925.

Olien, Diana Davids, and Roger M. Olien. *Oil in Texas: The Gusher Age, 1895-1945.* Austin: University of Texas Press, 2002.

Olsen, Stanley J. *Fossil Mammals of Florida.* Special Publication No. 6. Tallahassee: Florida Geological Survey, 1959. See also: http://www.intersurf.com/-chalcedony/Basilosaurus1.html.

Plummer, E. W. "Oil Town." *Monroe Morning World,* April 14, 1963.

Rister, Carl Coke. *Oil! Titan of the Southwest.* Norman: University of Oklahoma Press, 1949.

Rundell, Walter, Jr. *Early Texas Oil, A Photographic History, 1966-1936.* College Station: Texas A&M Press, 1977.

Schiebout, Judith A. "Montomery Landing and the Montgomery Landing Project (1978-1982)." In *Montgomery Landing Site, Marine Eocene (Jackson) of Central Louisiana,* edited by Judith A. Schiebout and William van den Bold, 5-34. Baton Rouge: Thirty-Sixth Annual Meeting of the Gulf Coast Association of Geological Societies, 1986.

Schlanger, Harry P. *The Origins of Petroleum: A Look at the Inorganic Abiotic and Organic Fossil Fuels Theories,* 2008. http://geologyecology.suite101.com/article.cfm/theoriesonoriginofpetroleum.

Shaw, J. A. "A Brief Survey of the Mineral Resources of Louisiana." *Louisiana Department of Conservation, General Minerals Bulletin No. 22* (1933): 33-125.

SONRIS (Strategic Online Natural Resources Information System, Louisiana Department of Natural Resources). 2000. http://sonris-www.dnr.state.la.us/sonlite.htm.

Teas, L. P. "Tertiary Production." In *Petroleum Development and Technology in 1926.* American Institute of Minerals, Metals, and Engineering, 1927, 681-84.

Wall, Juanita F. "Oil Boom Days in Tullos: 1923 to 1983, A Look at a Sixty-Year Span." *Jena Times/Olla-Tullos Signal,* April 6, 1983.

Wallace, Joseph. *The Rise and Fall of the Dinosaur.* New York: Gallery Books, 1987.

Weaver, Bobby. Introduction to *Roughnecks, Drillers, and Tool Pushers: Thirty-Three Years in the Oil Fields,* by Gerald Lynch, ix-xiv. Austin: University of Texas Press, 1987.

Williams, Cecil. "When Tullos Was an Untamed Oil Town." *Alexandria Daily Town Talk,* October 24, 1976.

Winberry, Emily Russell. "1950s: A Kid of the Firefly Fifties"; "The Sixties: A Decade of Changes"; "The 1970s: The Age of Aquarius"; "The 1980s: The Decade of the Small Businesses"; "1990s: Can You Go Home Again?" In *A History of the Town of Olla, 1830-1995.* Olla, LA: Privately printed, 1995.

Index